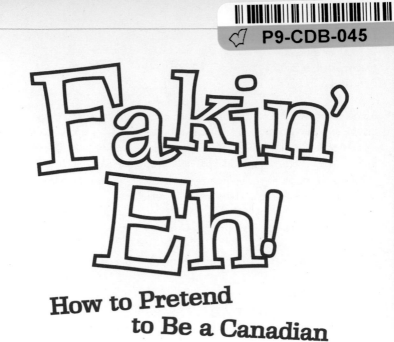

Fakin' Eh!

How to Pretend to Be a Canadian

Dan de Figueiredo

BLUE
BIKE
BOOKS

The Publisher: Blue Bike Books

Library and Archives Canada Cataloguing in Publication

De Figueiredo, Dan,
    Fakin' eh! : how to pretend to be a Canadian / Dan de Figueiredo;
illustrator: Roger Garcia.

ISBN-13: 978-0-9739116-3-3
ISBN-10: 0-9739116-3-8

    1. National characteristics, Canadian—Humor. 2. Canada—Humor.
3. Canadian wit and humor (English). I. Garcia, Roger, 1976– II. Title.

FC97.D43 2007   971.002'07   C2006-906407-5

Project Director: Nicholle Carrière
Illustrations: Roger Garcia
Cover Image: Roger Garcia

We acknowledge the financial support of the Alberta Foundation for
the Arts for our publishing program.

PC: P5

CONTENTS

DEDICATION

For the fake Canadian in everyone.

And for Paul and Simon, the rocks of my world, neither of whom was born in Canada...

...And thank God for that!

ACKNOWLEDGEMENTS

Fakin' My Way Through My Acknowledgements

Writing a book, though for the most part a solitary act, is never accomplished in a vacuum—though it has been known to happen inside a dryer, a refrigerator and, on special occasions, within the confines of a washing machine during the spin cycle. This is the point where I would generally insert a "just kidding" remark; however, the previous statement is, in fact, true.

But none of that has anything to do with my writing of this particular book—except that I did not accomplish the writing of this book while in a vacuum. I wrote all of this book, save for a few bits and pieces (which of course means not all of it), while sitting at a drafting table in my home office on the 22nd floor of the co-ownership building where I live. My desk, or should I say drafting table/desk, is situated in front of a window that looks west across Yonge Street, Bay Street and the greenery and jumble of the academic buildings of the University of Toronto. I have been advised by law enforcement not to get more specific than this about my location for fear of alerting stalkers, gawkers or groupies, especially since this book will be available in the U.S. market, where there are a lot more nuts! I say that with the utmost respect for the United States and its nuts.

I could not have accomplished the writing of this book without my desk/drafting table, my window or my 22nd floor co-ownership unit. I must thank all of these inanimate objects for their assistance. While I'm at it, I should also thank my computer for storing my words, my colour monitor for allowing me to see my words in black and white, the oh-so-many yellow-lined pads of paper, reams of eight-and-a-half by eleven white sheets, various pens, a few pencils and several yellow and blue highlighters for their input along with allowing me to nervously chew them. I would also be remiss in not thanking my chair and my highly cooperative, dedicated computer technician, who keeps me up and running, computer-wise, if not on the cutting edge in terms of software, hardware and performance ability. As I always tell him, "That's fine, it's not a race, it's all about the journey." And God knows, someone as easily distracted as me absolutely loves a detour. Thanks for the detours, computer tech guy whose name I can't quite remember or pronounce. However, I cannot in good conscience bring myself to thank Microsoft despite using many of their products. They're EVIL… especially that paperclip guy!

Now, I come to thanking the most important, and generally speaking, more animate beings that occupy my world. This is where things get a bit tricky for me, because people always judge the order in which their names appear, and even if they don't ask outright, they often wonder why he, she or it was thanked before them. My rule of thumb here is to go in an order that is truly random. Then people can't really figure out if first thanked or last is most important. Because let's face it, you are all extremely important to me!

I must thank my publisher for publishing my words, and being so supportive of my "unique" voice. I also have to thank that spirited and inventive game show I just finished working on for helping me to clear away debt, for giving me all those nifty answers (yes, no, yes, no, yes, no), but especially for giving me the financial stability necessary to write a book of this calibre. Who needs government grants when TV game shows are throwing away money? Who indeed?

Along with my publisher I also have to thank my editor, who allowed my voice to come through, redirected my excited but confused thoughts, and at times said, "Whoa, whoa, whoa!

Which language are you writing in again?" As well, I must thank Roger Garcia, the man who drew all the snappy illustrations in this book. They say a picture is worth a thousand words, and I say a wacky drawing is worth double that… especially if I can write fewer words. But even if that's not true, the illustrations are great!

I have to thank Simon. He's the dog that sits here with me constantly, sighs when I'm not paying him enough attention and daily reminds me that I do not co-own him—he owns me! I can't really thank him for being my co-writer, but I do thank him for being my co-pilot. He contributes to my writing in a great many ways. He's got a sore paw right now, so I have to lay it on extra thick here. Done.

My parents, Sharon and Bob Lindsay, as well as my mother-in-law, Gena Figueiredo, contribute with their interest, their stories, their food, their conversation, their advice, their ongoing presence and with the fact that they "know" me. And, I'm glad they do.

My extended family—Tilburys, Toomeys, Staits, Lindsays, Bigelows and Dilkses—have helped me on this one in ways that they will not have a clue about—unless they read the entire book. They provided the early models on which my construct of the idealized Canadian is based. If they read this paragraph, they will know my sense of humour is influenced by theirs…or at least they'll take some credit for it!

Other individuals, groups and objects that have helped me on this one include BBC News; CBC News; CTV.ca; the Canadian Encyclopaedia; Random House; the Oxford Dictionary of Canadian English; the late Dick Benner, an American-born writer and my friend, for telling me I was funny and I should write that way; the Dixie Chicks for their inspired music and their amazing strength of will; the city of Toronto, which I proudly call my home; and the *Toronto Star* newspaper, especially for the Sunday edition. I must also thank the United States of America and its people for being stable, friendly and easy to laugh with and at. And, I cannot forget to thank Canada and Canadians for being well meaning, compassionate and way less than perfect or ideal. Canada truly is a country where one can learn and grow, make mistakes and get a second chance, and yet it still produces some of the worst television known to man! Oh, yeah, it's stinky!

I know I said my acknowledgements were randomly ordered, but I break that rule for this last one since it is the most important of all. It's for Paul, who helps me every day and in every way—except in loading the dishwasher. He's not so good at that. But in every other way. This is no joke. Thanks!

Oh, and I almost forgot. Thanks, God. Still doing a bang-up job there, bud!

INTRODUCTION

It is perhaps a peculiar thing to think that a Canadian like myself would want to help Americans like you to pretend to be a Canadian like myself. Well, hold on there, Sparky! You're getting a bit ahead of yourself. I sincerely doubt that any of you will ever approximate being even one-tenth as close to truly Canadian as me. My intention in writing this here book (to use your vernacular) is to get you to a place that could approximate being some kind of Canadian—a lesser Canadian than me, but one somehow acceptable by Canadian standards.

Now, just what constitutes Canadian standards is a complex, hitherto almost unknowable framework of constructs, means tests and knowing glances that is both quite broad and supremely vague. Unless you are an at-par Canadian like myself, you will probably not ever be able to understand.

Just kidding!

The above paragraphs are an example of Canadian condescension with just a twist of British arrogance thrown in for good measure. Although Canadians might suggest they are never condescending, they are using condescension when they say it. And although we claim that we abhor British arrogance, we are more than a little familiar with it and know how to use it.

I know both these constructs very well. And I know how to speak, write and/or keep these to myself, depending on the situation I am in. That, my good friends, is what makes me eminently qualified to advise you on how to pretend to be Canadian. As someone who was born, brought up and has lived most of his life in Canada, who could better advise you on what makes a Canadian? Perhaps the only better advisor might be someone who also lived among you Americans, has had much contact with you Americans and was indoctrinated into your American culture by your movies, music and especially your American television. You can also count me in that camp.

I was born and grew up in Hamilton, Ontario, Canada—a steel town less than an hour's drive from the U.S. border at Niagara Falls. Hamilton has been called the Pittsburgh of Canada. I have been to Pittsburgh. Why any place would want to be called the Pittsburgh of Canada, or of anywhere, perhaps says a whole lot more about a Canadian attitude that makes us just grateful to be noticed than it does about the lovely place where I spent the formative years of my life. Or perhaps not. I mean, Hamilton is, and always has been, if not beautiful, definitely noticeable…and often smellable.

When I was an infant, my parents had the grand notion that living south of the border—even south of the Pittsburgh of the United States—would be better, "so they loaded up the truck, and we moved to Beverly…Hills that is, swimmin' pools, movie stars." Actually, they moved us to a largely industrial section of Los Angeles south of Beverly called Torrance. Perhaps it could be best described as the Pittsburgh of California. After about a year of that fun, we were all deported. That really was the first indication I had that perhaps Canadians and Americans weren't one and the same. Though how the INS discovered we were not American is beyond me. Perhaps it was the way we said out and about—*owt* and *uhbowt*. It could also have been how we said milk—*melk*.

The origins of this book really stem from the second time I was living in the United States. The roots can be pinpointed to that infamous date: September 11, 2001. I had been living in Bethesda, Maryland, on and off for almost a year. Bethesda is a suburb of Washington, DC—cozy, quiet and disturbingly friendly by Canadian standards. People actually say hello to each other, even good morning, but not just occasionally and to people they know, but all the time and to complete strangers. It is definitely disturbingly friendly or perhaps excessively intrusive by Canadian standards. (Since originally writing the previous sentence I have been informed by my editor and my mother that people in parts of Canada—Hamilton Mountain and the Prairies—do, in fact, mirror the disturbingly friendly or excessively intrusive greetings of the "folks" of Bethesda, Maryland. Perhaps. Or perhaps they just wish, hope and are willing to fib just a bit to put a sunnier face on their parts of Canada. But now I have digressed into a debate when I was intending to put forward the origins of this book.) Bethesda isn't exactly where this book came from, although it did have a small hand in it...whether it was friendly by Canadian standards or not.

In the events and aftermath of 9-11, this book began. The horror, the tragedy and even the triumph of the collective human spirit that emerged that day made me feel as though I was one with the people of the United States. As the days and weeks moved forward, grief moved to revenge. The Baltimore Ravens team flags disappeared from cars and were replaced by American flags. The government and peoples' attitudes moved to, "If you're not with us, you're agin' us." I realized then that I was not one of you, nor was I one with you.

The odd thing that happened, or at least surprised me, was that many of you were also not okay with the direction things had moved in those weeks and months after 9-11. Some of you were appalled, some disheartened, some truly embarrassed. Mind you, those of you who fell into that camp were much fewer in number and much quieter still. You are probably more Democrat in terms of party affiliation, perhaps even fruitily French from a Karl Rove–Republican Party standpoint. So, vive les Freedom Fries libre!

As I extricated myself from my U.S. entanglement, I faced a number of twists and turns, bumps and grinds in my life. I came face to face with a true sociopath and may have even encountered evil—not Microsoft evil, though. But all of that is for another story, perhaps even a soap opera. While all of that living, being and moving was going on, I put my knowledge of the "Americans who didn't want to be Americans" in the back of my mind.

It wasn't until I was back working and living in Toronto and walking my dog Simon that I thought about my out-of-place or displaced American brethren again. You see, Simon is a small, white dog who was born in the United States. He was a stray, but nevertheless he is like many Americans: in your face, not afraid to ask for what he wants and not at all into waiting his turn. He's also got a few prejudices that I'm not going to go into. He's American through and through.

But the odd thing about Simon's American heritage and attitude is that back in Canada people don't seem to notice. Most Canadians don't recognize his American tendencies. They are surprised to learn that he is American. They think he's just another dog—just another Canadian-born dog.

Eureka!

Seeing Simon's ruse play out, I seized on an idea. What if Simon was the key to helping all stray Americans live out happy, well-adjusted lives? What if, indeed! Could he be a model for all Americans who no longer felt akin to their countrymen and their government? What if, instead of waiting for their country to return to sanity, I could help Americans to help themselves by giving them a way to fake their way through being Canadian? Could any American who wanted to be just like my American-born dog Simon?

I wasn't sure.

But using Simon as my model, I set about designing a system— a way for all desperate Americans to become fake Canadians. And, I remember this breakthrough moment as clear as a smog-free day in Hamilton or Pittsburgh. I was walking Simon in the park at the time that this stroke of genius came to me. I stopped dead in my tracks and repeated an oft-used American sit-com cliché: "Ya know, it's so crazy it just might work!" After I repeated that phrase out loud, I had no more doubts. I had my answer. I knew it would work.

And that, my friends, is how this all began.

So, read on and I will show you the way. The way to Fakin' Eh!

Part 1
In the Beginning, Eh!

*It's been said that a Canadian is someone who can
make love in a canoe...
So, I guess a fake Canadian is someone who
actually tries it.*

Anonymous

*From: The Big Book of Fake Canadian Quotes...
Okay, It's A Small Book*

CHAPTER ONE

HOW TO USE THIS FAKIN' EH! BOOK
(THE PREAMBLE, EH!)

In the beginning, there is always a blank piece of paper—at least if you are a writer, which I am. One of the most difficult things for me is to figure out the audience I am writing for and thus where to start. The oft-quoted phrase "start at the beginning" may seem simple enough, but it is not really. I want to start with you, my friends, for this journey you have chosen to take will not be easy. But I commend you for trying. I don't envy the hurdles you will encounter or the difficulties you will put yourself through—not the least of which will be the vomit-inducing punch to the delicate bits that you must be taking in going from a nation that screams "WE ARE THE BEST!" to a nation that mumbles, perhaps whispers with a coy smile, "We're okay, fine, not too bad, thank you very much for asking."

With that in mind and pushing forward, please know that what follows is written with the utmost respect, even though it may not seem so at first. My intention in writing this self-help book is do just that—guide you in helping yourself. But I also intend to help the broadest spectrum of people who want my help. In covering material for the broadest spectrum, I have to be concerned that I may alienate some of you as you may think I am being condescending. Please do not be concerned over whether I am condescending. I am. Let's face it, I am the teacher, you are the pupil and you have a lot to learn. Those of you who may feel alienated or angered by the simplistic nature of my words should relish the fact that you feel condescended to, whereas others are busily trying to learn and keep up with all of the new, unusual and interesting Canadian information, and don't see the condescension. The great equalizer about this book is that eventually you won't feel my condescension either. It will still be there, but you won't feel it. You too will eventually feel the thrill of learning Canadian as the full-on force of my condescension disappears behind your learning curve.

Remember also that different people have different "smarts." There are book smarts, street smarts and even financial smarts—which I clearly don't have since I have chosen to be a writer. So we need to be patient and gracious enough to allow for those with fewer wits to catch up to our level. Hopefully, you can be amused and entertained by my earliest and most basic teachings until that eventually transforms into the thrill of learning from me, the master.

Please read with gusto, all the while realizing that you should take all the information in this book in the same way that I wrote it—with tongue firmly planted in cheek.

Who Should Use Fakin' Eh!

This book is designed to help Americans. And by "Americans," I mean people who are citizens of the United States of America. Sometimes people from other parts of the Americas (North America, Central America, South America and the Caribbean)

are referred to by outsiders as Americans. This book is not designed for their use, although it is not forbidden. And, by the way, the only people who actually call themselves Americans are people from the United States of America, or I suppose people who are pretending to be from there. The rest of us who live in the Americas are absolutely fine with the fact that citizens of the United States use this blanket term to describe themselves, as if they are the only people who live in the Americas at all. Whatever.

So, as I wrote earlier, this book was designed and written with the express purpose of helping Americans—helping them to become fake Canadians. Now, I know what many people may be thinking. What God-fearing "True" American would ever be interested in pretending to be Canadian? Here's a list:

- Americans travelling in foreign lands (places other than the United States of America) who do not want to be singled out and ridiculed or worse just because they live in the land of the free and the home of the brave;

- American researchers who wish to try and understand their northern neighbour (or southern neighbour if they live in Alaska, or northeastern neighbour if they live in Hawaii);

- American business people who want to better figure out the mindset of the people of their country's largest trading partner and thus be able to sell more of their "Great American Stuff" to Canadian consumers;

- American military personnel wishing not to become cannon fodder in a war that never seems to end and that seemingly does not have a reasonable plan for ending;

- American convicts, criminals and tax evaders wishing to elude capture (although I would prefer that these people not use my book);

- A less-than-stellar President, who at the end of his second term wants to slip unnoticed out of the country he's run into the ground and fears no other country will accept him because he's alienated the world except for Israel, and God knows he's not going to live in that war zone because his wife, a former school teacher similar in personality to the colour beige, just won't have it.

There are several other types of people who might be interested in using this book. They are people who are not Americans, although, as I've said the book was not designed for their use. They include:

- Canadians who have in some sense lost their way and want a refresher on what it will take to fake their way back into being Canadian (although I would prefer that ex-pat Canadians who are disgraced or convicted ex-CEOs of multinational corporations also not use this book);

- Canadian politicians who want to confirm that their reading of Canadians is correct, but are too close to them and need an unbiased source for confirmation;

- Reviewers, journalists, reality TV producers or documentary filmmakers who wish to see how well my techniques work;

- People who love an adventure and have tried all the bungee, rock and parachute kinds of adventures known to humans, but STILL WANT MORE!

If you are some other kind of foreign national who wants to become Canadian, you needn't follow the techniques outlined in this book. The ideas contained here might be a fun introduction to Canada, but really you should pick up my other book, *How To Immigrate To Canada with One Phone Call and Less than Fifty Bucks*. It's a classic, and although it's now out of print, it is available in a great many places if you really want to get your hands on it! Wink, wink, wink…You know what I mean.

It's also Organized, Eh!

Fakin' Eh!—that's this book you are currently reading—is divided into three very nicely organized and illustrated parts.

Part One is known as "In the Beginning, Eh!" It's the part you are currently reading and have just about completed. It sets up the whole book and tells you how to go about reading it.

Part Two is "Fakin' Eh, The Background." This is the largest section of the book and is divided into a number of excellent, fun, informative and hilariously illustrated chapters. It's the section that will give you the low-down on Canada and Canadians—how we look, think and act, our history, geography and everything else you might need to know in your pursuit of becoming a Fake Canadian. Keeners or those who want to excel at Fakin' Eh! will, of course, memorize every detail, but the rest of you will have a guide to coasting your way through Fakin' Eh! So, coast away!

Part Three is "Putting It All Together, Or How to Get Down With Your Fakin' Eh! Self." This is the section in which I tell you how to take all the information I've given to you so far, attach it to your own unique personality and build it into a believable Reasonable Facsimile of a Canadian. I'll teach you how to fake your way through any situation as a Canadian would. From faking your way across the border to job interviews, social situations and even dealing with intrusive media types, it's all here, it's all clear and some of it may sound a bit queer…but it works. This part will also explain how to practice and who to practice on.

For any one of the various types of people who want to use this book, my best "how to" advice is to read carefully, follow the instructions to the letter and memorize all the information. Before going full bore into being a fake Canadian, try out your techniques on others and see if you can pass. You might even want to take a weekend trip to some Canadian town close to the U.S. border, which would include 90–95 percent of the towns in Canada.

Whatever you do, go at this course and your transition into Fakin' Eh! society with a sense of humour and a two-fer in your trunk. Don't know what that means? By the end of this book you will. Now, fake away, eh!

CHAPTER TWO

SO, WHAT'S A CANADIAN ALL ABOUT, EH?

So, just what is the essence of being Canadian, and for your purposes the essence of being a fake Canadian? Well, that depends on whether you are a True Canadian, a Reasonable Facsimile of a Canadian or an Out-and-out Fake Canadian.

So, then, how does one answer the question what is the essence of being Canadian?

An **Out-and-out Fake Canadian** would quickly blurt out an answer to impress others—something like, "We all say, eh!" or "We're all nice!" or "We all love hockey!" Of course, this Out-and-out Fake Canadian would be revealed as a fake as much for the assertions of what we "all" say, "all" are or "all" love as from the manner in which the reply was voiced. You probably have no idea of what I am talking about, so read on.

A **True Canadian** would never blurt out an answer like an Out-and-out Fake Canadian. A True Canadian would ponder, think, perhaps even fart before forming a Royal Commission (the Canadian version of a governmental investigation) to study the question and come up with a long list of answers, none of which would be definitive, conclusive or be able to stand alone as the answer to what is the essence of being Canadian.

A **Reasonable Facsimile of a Canadian** would take some time, think, ponder for a shorter period of time, maybe even squeeze out a fart or titter and then perhaps come up with three plausible responses to the question. However, the Reasonable Facsimile of a Canadian would never blurt out an answer first or blurt out an answer at all with the intention of fitting in, looking smart or impressing others.

So, are you getting the essence of being or faking being a Canadian now? I don't see any hands, so that must mean you are getting it. Right? I still don't see any hands other than my own, which is probably because I'm writing this chapter months or even years before you are reading it. So let me continue.

Being Canadian isn't easy to understand, grasp or even fathom, unless you were born into it. It's an age-old question that has been asked since time immemorial—or at least since 1867, which for those of us alive today may as well be time immemorial because it was quite a long time ago and is very hard to grasp unless you have really big hands and the ability to travel through time. We, as True Canadians, have mastered this ability, but we don't like to boast about it. So let's just agree that figuring out the essence of being Canadian is something that has been pondered since time immemorial, where time is, well, the distance between now and immemorial, and immemorial is 1867.

Why 1867? Because that is the date when Canada became a nation—or at least a dominion, which isn't quite a nation, but isn't a colony, a state or a province either. Anyway, I'll explain that in the chapter on history and politics and all that fun stuff. Your first piece of memorization should be this one: Canada was born as a nation (sort of) on July 1, 1867. Now, let's get back to the essence of being Canadian.

The essence of being Canadian, if you are still with me, can be found in the three types of responses from the beginning of this chapter. It is not about things said, things done or even things loved. The essence of being Canadian is, in fact, all about the "how." When I write "how," I do not mean the false word created by Hollywood for "Indians" to use as a greeting in various "Cowboy vs. Indian" movies. The "how" I am talking about is the how of manner. When I write manner, I do, in fact, mean politeness.

The response of the Out-and-out Fake Canadian is first, is definitive and is showy—showy because it is first and definitive. It is not thoughtful, correct or in the remotest sense framed in a polite manner. It is designed solely for the Out-and-out Fake Canadian to show off, command attention and not only achieve number one status, but also browbeat others into submission. It is there to say, "Look at me!" "Look how smart I am!" and "Look how much smarter I am than you!" That, my good friends, is not Canadian.

Canadians are suspicious of anyone who feels a need to show off. To us, such bravado does not brim with self-confidence, but instead reveals an inherent insecurity that suggests the exact opposite. People who are truly confident and at the top of their game in any situation or field should never have a need to show it. People who need to show their number one status are insecure about being number one and therefore are not number one. A well-adjusted, confident person has no need to get there first and has no need to beat others into submission with their one single proof-positive answer.

A True Canadian will be polite enough to let others respond first, listen to those responses and add his own thoughtful comments, which will never be hurtful, boastful or framed as the one true answer. That doesn't mean that Canadians do not disagree or have opinions. Believe it or not, we do. We just don't feel the need for others to always agree with our opinions or for us to disagree with theirs in a forceful, vehement or grandstanding manner. Instead, we'll wait until they leave the room and talk behind their backs. And, when they are back in the room, polite conversation will resume despite their earnest and heartfelt pleas in the name of democracy, freedom or non-oil-related interests.

That, my friends, is the essence of being Canadian—friendly, polite and non-confrontational in public, and mean, snide and condescending behind your back...especially if your back is American.

So, the best advice I can give you as you make your way through this course on pretending to be Canadian is don't be showy in any way. Learn the ins and outs of our history, politics, society, culture, words, phrases and geography, but never show in public how much you have learned. Never show off how much you know about Canada or Canadians, for that will tip us off that you are not one of us, or you are one of us that has gone awry and we will have to knock you off your boastful perch and bring you back down to size. We'll do it, too. Just look at the list of overachieving Canadians who have been brought down to size: Prime Minister Brian Mulroney, Conrad Black, Prime Minister Paul Martin, Prime Minister Joe Clark, Prime Minister Kim Campbell, Prime Minister John Turner, Prime Minister John Diefenbaker, sprinter Ben Johnson, Ben Johnson's coach Charlie Francis, The Canadian Airborne Regiment, WorldCom CEO Bernard Ebbers, Grey Owl (an ardent environmentalist who pretended to be a Native Canadian and turned out to be British), Prime Minister John A. Macdonald.

The list, my friends, goes on and on and will probably eventually include people like current Canadian Prime Minister Stephen Harper.

OR…

Maybe, just maybe, there is one other thing that captures the essence of being Canadian. It's something that has become recognized in recent years even by outsiders who despise us in other ways. Look at what right-wing pundits Ann Coulter and Bill O'Reilly said about us on Fox News in 2004:

Ann Coulter: Canada better hope the United States doesn't roll over one night and crush them. They are lucky we allow them to exist on the same continent as us. And you know why that is, don't ya? We all know why. It's their intoxicating aroma.

Bill O'Reilly: I know. There's just nothing like the scent of a Canadian, is there?

Ann Coulter: I've never encountered any other group of people like them.

Bill O'Reilly: It's true, they smell so damn good.

It's true, my eager young apprentices! We smell damn fine. And it's not our hair care products, or our soap, or even our perfumes and aftershaves. No sirree, it is the other inherent and unfakeable thing about us. As your American actor Al Pacino says about us, "Ooh-waaaa!" And our scent is not something easily duplicated. Like our non-showy nature, it is just inherently part of us.

But don't despair. Just shower often and you'll be there!

Part 2
Fakin' Eh! The Background

The state has no place in the bedrooms of the nation.
–Former Prime Minister Pierre Elliot Trudeau in
1967, when he was Minister of Justice

Ah, the background section. This is where we start to
build the new, improved, Canadian-like you. Fakin' eh!
The background includes all of the things most Canadians
know about their homeland—luckily for you, that isn't
much. If you study this background information—don't
just memorize, but live, breathe and really know it—
you'll be halfway to becoming a Reasonable Facsimile of
a Canadian. And, of course, never use this information to
show off...and always make sure you smell good!

CHAPTER THREE

THE BASICS, EH!

Canada is a really big place, especially if you try to walk from one ocean to another to another. That's right, three oceans! Not one, not two, but three! In your face, Australia!

What about other water? Ya know, the fresh kind? Well, we've got water, water everywhere. So much, in fact, that the low-flow toilet isn't even a consideration. We have the only super-high-volume toilets in the world. Every time we "go," a deluge flushes it away with the power, volume and misty spray of Niagara Falls—the Canadian falls, that is, not those tiny, sketchy and second-rate American falls. Okay, we don't really have those super-high-volume toilets, but we do waste a lot of water. And that's mainly because we can. Sorry!

Remember all that space I told you that we have? Well, most of it is also wasted. Not wasted, exactly, but not really used. Some parts of Canada are seldom (if ever) seen because, in terms of people, there are only about 32.5 million of us. Most of us are stuffed into towns and cities just a hop, skip, and a jump from the U.S. border. Which, as you may or may not know, is the

longest undefended border in the world. Why would we defend it? Come on in! Lots of room for everyone, which I believe is still the official slogan for our immigration department. Okay, it's not the official slogan, but it's definitely implied.

Some other things you may not know, but want to know—or let's face it—are just dying to know:

- We have a red and white flag with the ubiquitous maple leaf planted dead centre.

- We also have a coat of arms that has lions and a unicorn, a lot of maple leaves, a crown, a couple of flags and some other foliage, flowers and leftover stuff on it. (Though the problem with the coat of arms is that we were never given a coat or arms to put it on, so it remains stuffed into a desk drawer somewhere in Ottawa for safekeeping.)

Now we segue to Ottawa. Ottawa is our nation's capital. It used to be called Bytown, but the name was changed when unscrupulous lobbyists moved in, thinking the name implied that favours, votes and even senators could be bought with the right amounts of money. But clearly, these things could not be bought with money in this feisty logging berg. That could only be done with 'Ot,' which in Canadian terms means really big gifts like diamonds, gold mines and the Northwest Territories! Okay, not really. The name is derived from a local gang. Not really, again. The name actually comes from the local First Nations tribe, of which there are only a handful left, but a rich handful now that they have found their one true calling—casinos.

But Ottawa isn't our only city, believe it or not. In fact, Ottawa isn't even the biggest city…or second biggest…or third biggest. The biggest cities are Toronto, Montreal and Vancouver. Those three cities are each found in different provinces. You see, in Canada, we don't have states like you do in the United States. We have provinces and territories. There are reasons for having both provinces and territories, but you'll find that out later. Suffice it to say that Canada is made up of ten provinces and three territories—not counting Estotiland, of course, which many think is the fourth territory, at least on an imaginary and purely invisible plain. Of course, imaginary and invisible plains are not recognized in the Constitution, so at present we only count three territories.

Canada was originally founded by First Nations (Aboriginal) people, whose traditions suggest that they've been here forever. Archaeologists think Canada's Native peoples have been here for less than 30,000 years. But let's not quibble. They were certainly here before the English and the French, who swarmed in like locusts and took over with nary a regard for the locals. I believe America had some similar dealings with their First Nations people as well? Or maybe I'm wrong and everyone south of our border just got along!

Finally, in 1867, Canada came together as a nation that was called the Dominion of Canada. That eventually became too long for licence plates and bumper stickers, so the name is now officially just Canada. It's spelled the same way in both English and French, which is one of the few things that Canada's two largest linguistic groups can agree on.

"No, we can't!"

"Mon Dieu, non!"

Or perhaps we can't. But the spelling is actually the same whether we officially agree on it or not. I guess you've already guessed that we have two official languages: English and French.

The government settled on by Canadians was a Constitutional Monarchy, which basically means we retain the British Monarch as our head of state. We have a Governor General who represents the monarch in Canada and gives royal assent, which is just a rubber stamp needed to pass a bill.

The head of our government is called the Prime Minister, and he is the leader of the ruling party in the House of Commons. One gets to be Prime Minister by having the winning ticket in the National Lottery, which is held on December 31 at midnight. Tickets are $2 or a book of 10 for $15. Not really. Tickets are always free and issued to every citizen at birth…sorry, I meant at hatching! No, no, no. I must stop with the antics now. When you read about our government and politics later in Part Two, you'll see how one becomes Prime Minister…eeew! It doesn't necessarily involve slime.

In terms of religion, you probably already know that Canada is not what you'd call a "God-fearing" nation like the nation in which you live. We are, however, a "God-considering" nation, which basically means we worship, perhaps even believe in the One Almighty, the Two Mikeys or the Ancient Tree Wizard. It doesn't really matter who, what or where He or She is, most of us have some sort of religious beliefs. However, we do our worshipping when we feel like it, in our own quiet and personal way, and we keep it off the streets, out of the schools and government offices and in our homes and places of worship where it belongs. For the most part, that is…

Which brings us to sex. Yes, we do it! Often. And for long periods of time. Oh, yeah, we've got stamina. Not just with—hang on a second, this is getting just a bit personal. So, then let's talk about the gays. That's right, we have them, and we're not afraid of them, either. We don't just let our homosexuals marry; we encourage them to do so and to procreate as well. How else are we going to keep our birthrates high and our fun factor low? Besides, you know how competitive the "straights" are. When they see the birthrates of the gays on the rise, it really makes them get down to business—where business is sex, and getting down is, well, getting down!

We also play a bit differently than you down south. We don't have to brag about the fact that we invented hockey and baseball and basketball because clearly our winning track record in hockey speaks for itself. The other two were really just started as jokes, but we are glad you have taken them as your own. We also have a new game called Crushandkillball, which we think you might be interested in. And we have our own variation on

football, which allows your underachievers to play in a less competitive manner on a bigger field. It's nothing if not boring.

In terms of culture, we've, ah, got some. That's right! French, English and many other interesting ethnic groups make for an amazing meeting of world cultures in a mosaic of acceptance unlike the world has ever known. Despite this, or perhaps because of it, we make some of the worst films and television programs of any place on Earth, except maybe Andorra. Actually, I hear they have a nifty reality show there called *Where the Hell Are We?* so I must take back the derogatory remark I just made about the Andorrans. I'm really sorry.

Which brings me to "sorry." That's a word that we Canadians know how to say—and not mean. But we make people think we mean it sincerely, like when we feign interest by saying "wow," or "interesting," or "that's one way to go." There are a lot more of these words and phrases, too, that'll save your proverbial Fakin' Eh! butt, but I'm sorry to say you'll have to read the whole book to get a handle on all of our quaint little words and phrases. Actually, I'm not. Sorry, that is. Did you catch how I used the sorry, eh? And now, eh? Tricky, huh?

Other tricky phrases include bathroom and washroom, which we say instead of restroom, as is common in your country. You should also note that many words that end in "er" where you come from end in "re" up here, but they're pronounced the same in both places. I'm talking about words like "centre," which is "center" to you, or "kilometre," which is "mile" to you. Okay that's a bit different, but it does bring us to the metric system, which has been our official system of measure since the 1970s. Luckily, for you, the majority of the Canadian population still understands the imperial system, which is what you Americans use. In fact, most people probably only understand that one, so metric's not liable to trip you up. And if you're on a driving trip, you'll almost always think you've gotten there really fast because kilometres are so much smaller than miles.

A couple of other basics you need to know. Our monetary system is also metric—but don't worry about it because yours is as well. All it means really is that it is based on the dollar system. The only real difference is that Canadian money comes in many different colours and Queen Elizabeth II's face is on our coins. Oh, and there are no one- or two-dollar bills. Those are coins that you will affectionately come to know as "Bobs" and "Dougs." Not really. The dollar coins are often referred to as "loonies," and the two-dollar coins are usually called "toonies."

You'll also need to remember that our national anthem is "O Canada," but the words aren't that important because they changed awhile back, and no one can really remember what they are supposed to be. Just remember "true north strong and free" and "stand on guard for thee," and you'll do fine! You should also remember that the royal anthem, "God Save the Queen," is sometimes played. But this only happens in the deepest, darkest Tory conclaves, or when the Queen (or her representative) is nearby. So as a general rule, you won't have to worry about it.

What's a Tory conclave, you ask? It's like a church revival meeting without the revival—you know, people who all have their butt cheeks tightly clamped and haven't got a progressive thought in their heads! No, really, I'm not joking this time. Tory(ies) is a colloquial term used to describe people who are supporters of the Conservative political party. Their counterparts in the Liberal party are called Grits. There are other political parties in Canada, which include the NDP (New Democratic Party), which is more socialist than the Liberal party, and the Bloc Québecois party, which is the federal version of the separatist Parti Québecois from the province of Québec. I know what you're thinking: "How do you have a federal separatist party?" I don't know. None of us know. But we do.

The last basic thing you need to know is that Canada's official motto is "A Mari Usque Ad Mare," which translated from Latin basically means, "A Beaver in Every Pot!" Not really. It actually means "from sea to sea," but we don't much use it anymore because it left out the third sea…In your face, Australia!

CHAPTER FOUR

OWT AND UHBOWT IN THE FAKIN' EH! PLACE, EH!

I must confess this before I die. We never actually went there—across the Great Plains, through the Rockies or to the Pacific Ocean. Ack! There was this Metis princess named Shirley, you see. I met her somewhere west of Fort Garry. I just couldn't leave her. She did this thing with her tongue. Shirley's brother was a great storyteller. He gave me all the information I needed to claim that I was the first white man to reach the Pacific Ocean by land north of Mexico. What I'm trying to say is that my life's great accomplishment is entirely made up. Ack! Gurgle, gurgle, gurgle. Ahhhhhh!

–Tabloid account of what Alexander MacKenzie said on his deathbed, as reported by Meriwether Lewis and William Clark

In your quest to become a Reasonable Facsimile of a Canadian, you are going to need to know something about Canadian geography, though not that much. However, it will be more than what you know about your own country's geography, if I am to believe what I have read about what you know about where you live. I, like most intelligent Canadians…(Which does not mean to imply that most Canadians are intelligent. There are as many dummies per capita in this country as there are in yours. One only needs look at our political ranks to prove this.) But as I was saying, I, like most intelligent Canadians, don't like to believe hype. However, my years of living in Washington, DC, do indeed lead me to believe that you, as Americans, are a people who are geographically challenged. When I say, with the utmost respect, that you are geographically challenged, what I really mean is that you really don't know where you live:

whether that is on terra firma or inside the hole of a rolling doughnut (that's donut to you). The correct answer to where you live in the broadest sense is terra firma—meaning Earth. You do not in fact live inside the hole of a rolling doughnut.

What I began to write at the beginning of this chapter was that you are going to have to know something about Canadian geography in order to pass as a Reasonable Facsimile of a Canadian. So here goes.

CANADA

Canada is a very large place. In fact, it is the second largest country in the world, behind only Russia in terms of area. But I'll bet you didn't know that. Most maps and satellite images of North America skew the visual to make it look as though the United States is the largest part of North America. One explanation for this is that satellite images of North America come from satellites that travel closer to the equator than to the North Pole, so satellite images lop off the top part of Canada or skew the photos by the angle from where they are taken—making things look bigger at the bottom and smaller at the top. I suspect these explanations are correct, although some might suggest that the American companies that create these images have ulterior motives for their skewed interpretations. I really have no opinion on this.

As I was saying, Canada is a large place full of natural resources, although not that full of people. Although according to the CIA World Fact Book, Canada is only "somewhat bigger than the United States." Somewhat is an ill-defined term that sounds like a child saying, "Oh, yeah!" or "So what?" or even "You and what army?" In the case of Canada, that would be the army of the U.S., so let's get back to geography.

One big thing you may want to remember is that the longest undefended border in the world is the one between Canada and the United States, which runs 6416 kilometres (4000 miles). That is actually the southern border of Canada, which butts up against the northern border of the contiguous United States, or the lower 48 as they are often called. Canada also borders the state of Alaska with a 2500-kilometre (1500-mile) undefended border. So the total undefended border between Canada and the United States is a whopping 8893 kilometres (5500 miles)! Now, the numbers here aren't that important except to paint a very large picture with Picasso-like noses that appear very much out of place.

You should also remember some other large things. Mount Logan is Canada's tallest mountain. We share four out of the five Great Lakes with the United States—Superior, Huron, Erie and Ontario. Apparently, America got greedy when it came to the fifth Great Lake (Michigan), which it keeps entirely for itself. These lakes along with the St. Lawrence River make up the largest part of the border with the province of Ontario. Other lakes you may want to make note of are Great Bear Lake, Great Slave Lake and Lake Winnipeg, You don't really have to remember where any of these are located, just that they are within Canada. Okay, perhaps it's best to also know that Lake Winnipeg is in the province of Manitoba.

This brings us to the provinces—or more correctly, the provinces and territories—which make up our political divisions in much the same way that you in the United States have states.

Canada has 10 provinces and three territories. The difference between what makes a province and what makes a territory is largely unknown to the Canadian populace. Most people believe it's that territories are sparsely populated, and you may use this explanation. It will not get you in trouble. However, the real explanation, which you would not want to use for fear of showing off, has more to do with control. The federal government in Ottawa has more control over the territories and their natural resources than it does over those of the provinces. A good example of this control is that for most of my life there were just two territories: Yukon and the Northwest Territories. As of 1999, the Northwest Territories was subdivided in two, much like my mother used to cut a peanut butter and jam sandwich into two and give half to me and half to my older brother. The western half is still called the Northwest Territories, despite no longer being either the most northerly or the most westerly territory. The eastern half was renamed Nunavut.

This subdivision of the Northwest Territories has happened before. Much of the western half of Canada was once part of the Northwest Territories before it was subdivided into the provinces of Manitoba, Saskatchewan and Alberta as well as Yukon territory. This, as I said, is the difference between provinces and territory—control. The federal government will on occasion divide or sub-divide territories, whereas they dare not do so with provinces. Otherwise, I do believe the federal government would have divided a couple or more of the provinces in order to get the rights to their natural resources and/or to teach a lesson or two to some squawking politicians and redneck citizens!

The Thirteen

One final note about provinces and territories. If you add them all up, there are 13—10 provinces and three territories. This has been the case ever since 1999. The number 13 is, of course, thought to be an unlucky number. Since 1999, an awful lot of bad luck has befallen Canada. Just look:

- Wayne Gretzky retired from hockey, so we had to suffer through seeing yet another overpaid crybaby of an athlete in tears.

- Walkerton, Ontario, suffered a deadly *E. coli* outbreak, which proved a Conservative government didn't care a fig for its people as long as it was slashing taxes and services.

- Former Liberal Prime Minister Pierre Trudeau died, and from then on, we've had to suffer through daily reports about what his wacky ex-wife and incredibly uninteresting, untalented and dimwitted children are doing.

- George Bush became President of the United States, and although that's not directly bad luck to Canada, it has proved tragic for the world at large.

- 9-11

- Ben Mulroney, son of former Prime Minister Brian Mulroney, began appearing on television as a host on CTV. Soon he became the host of all that is Canadian TV. Hasn't the public suffered enough at the hands of the Mulroney clan?

BEN MULRONEY

- Four Canadian soldiers were killed in Afghanistan by American military pilots in a friendly fire incident, foreshadowing what was to come for Canada's military in Afghanistan.

- SARS (Severe Acute Respiratory Syndrome) hit Toronto, causing illness and death and making Canada's largest city famous, a pariah and a no-fly zone for the world, although it did lead to the demise of dim-witted Mayor Mel "Boil Me in a Pot in Africa" Lastman.

- Mad Cow Disease hit the cattle set in Alberta (and beef cows as well).

- Canada lost to the U.S. in the 2004 World Junior Hockey Championships—is Armageddon next?

- Britain sold Canada a bunch of used submarines, and one caught fire and killed a crewman, all because salt water dripped inside it. Britain said ,"Hey, it's an as-is sale. They were jolly alright when we sold them to you."

- Fox News is allowed to be broadcast in Canada in the same year that President George W. Bush visits Ottawa. One of the four horsemen is seen near Megiddo, Israel.

- Belinda Stronach was elected a Member of Parliament as a Conservative, later became a Liberal and still later was re-elected, proving Canada is no slouch when it comes to producing rich-girl Paris Hilton clones.

- Stephen Harper became Prime Minster of Canada, and almost immediately, his party's collective brains began falling out as he and his cronies fawned at the feet of U.S. President George W. Bush.

- A terrorism plot by a gang of inept teenagers was broken up in Toronto. Colonel Klink, of Hogan's Heroes fame, was thought to be the mastermind.

- Canadian record producer David Foster was awarded the Order of Canada. Canadians yawned in collective lack of interest. Then our yawns turned to alarm when we began to wonder, "What's next? Will we have to let Celine Dion back into the country?"

If you're not sure about the significance of any of these unbelievable tragedies that have befallen Canada, you can look them up. They're all true. Now, after reading about all of these significantly horrible events, does anyone think that bad luck hasn't befallen us since 1999, when we became "The Thirteen"? I think we need to rid ourselves of all the bad luck that is and has become associated with "The Thirteen." We should perhaps add a province or a territory or lose one? You know, Québec is an awfully big place. What about subdividing it? Or perhaps we should finally set tiny Prince Edward Island adrift, or alternately, join it to Nova Scotia or New Brunswick? Maybe Labrador should become its own province or territory? I'm not sure what will work best, but we have to lose the status and grief that go with "The Thirteen." I mean, come on people! Look what happened to the original 13 colonies. Yes they won their revolution, but they became the United States. We don't want that now, do we?

THE TERRITORIES

Yukon

Yukon is the most westerly of the territories and should be referred to as Yukon, not *the* Yukon, despite the fact that most Canadians call it the Yukon. The official name is Yukon. It is located north of British Columbia, east of Alaska and west of the Northwest Territories. Yes, despite the Northwest Territories' name, Yukon is located west of it. Yukon's two major cities are Dawson and the capital, Whitehorse. Most Canadians have never visited Yukon, so your knowledge of the territory can be minimal: its location, the two major cities (which are not too

major when it comes to world city size) and the fact that Canada's largest mountain, Mount Logan, is found here. It's also safe to say it's cold there during the very long winters and not quite warm in the week that they call summer...okay, it may be a little longer than a week.

The Northwest Territories

The Northwest Territories are now sandwiched between Yukon to the west, Nunavut to the north and east and British Columbia, Alberta and Saskatchewan to the south. Except for British Columbia, all of the rest of these provinces and territories as well as parts of the provinces of Ontario and Québec used to be part of the Northwest Territories. The lesson seems to be that if a territory gets too big for its britches, the federal government will knock it down to size. The Northwest Territories, which is now neither north nor west, has never learned this lesson. It's been cut to pieces over and over again. I think that because of all of this unfortunate subdividing, it's time for a name change for the NWT. Perhaps it should be called "This Could Happen to You Land, So Just Watch It, Alberta!" or if that's too

long, "NWT We Hardly Knew You," or as a last resort, "You Want a Piece of Me? Okay, Take It." The two major communities in the Northwest Territories are Yellowknife—not actually named for a dispute over a gold-plated cutting utensil—and Inuvik, pronounced *ih-new-vik*. And those two big lakes I mentioned earlier in the chapter, Great Bear Lake and Great Slave Lake? They can be found within the NWT, or at least for now, until the next subdivision happens. I think that lobotomy is scheduled for just after the next federal election. The new territory will be called Stephen Harper Land, or the Land of the Lost, or some such thing.

Nunavut

Nunavut is Canada's newest territory. It came into existence on April 1, 1999. The name, Nunavut, means, "Look At the Cool Land They Gave Us, Eh!" Actually, it means "Our Land" in Inuktitut, which is the Inuit language. At last count, there were some 29,000 shivering people in this vast land, which makes up the largest part of Canada and includes the North Pole. About

85 percent of the inhabitants are Inuit people. Santa Claus and his elves and reindeer make up the rest, I guess. The capital city—actually the only darn city in the whole territory—is Iqaluit *(ih-cal-ooh-wheat)*, which is at the southeastern end of Baffin Island. Iqaluit used to be called Frobisher Bay, but was renamed after a vote by inhabitants. So goes progress, history and Canada. Much of Nunuvut is above the tree line, which means, well, no trees. Easier for unscrupulous mining companies to strip mine, I guess. Not that there are any unscrupulous anythings in Canada. I've said enough.

ON TO THE PROVINCES

There are 10 provinces, as I've written previously, and you should probably know at least their names and their capitals, though many Canadians get mixed up when it comes to the names of some of the provincial capitals…especially those of Newfoundland and New Brunswick…Just wait for it, and you'll see why!

The Atlantic Provinces

These are the four provinces that are on Canada's Atlantic Coast: Newfoundland and Labrador, Nova Scotia, Prince Edward Island and New Brunswick.

Newfoundland OR Newfoundland and Labrador?

Here's the thing about Canada's easternmost province: It's got one or two names depending on who you're talking to. The Canadian constitution officially calls it Newfoundland, but the province officially calls itself Newfoundland and Labrador. Canadians know that the province is made up of the island of Newfoundland and the mainland piece called Labrador, but generally speaking, we all just call it Newfoundland. Why? Probably because Labrador doesn't have that many residents compared to Newfoundland. It's also probably because it's easier to tell a joke about Newfies than it is to tell one about Newfie-Labradorans. Yes, Canadians, like people of other countries, pick at least one part of our country to make fun of. For the longest time it was Newfoundland, mocked in the form of Newfie jokes, which are basically a variation on blonde jokes except that they feature a Newfie. An example:

"Have you heard about the Newfie who died ice fishing?"

"No. What happened?"

"He got run over by a Zamboni."

(For those of you who don't know what a Zamboni is, it is the machine that cleans the ice at a hockey rink.)

In the United States, your variation on the Newfie joke might be the redneck joke. In Portugal, as another example, they make fun of the people who come from a region called Alentejo, although in Portugal, the Alentejano being run over

by a Zamboni doesn't really translate as funny. It's more tragic and embarrassing really.

The interesting thing about Newfoundlanders being the butt of jokes is that the joke's really on the rest of Canada. Why? Because the rest of Canada has a really big butt! Not really. It's because Newfoundlanders are probably the funniest group of people in Canada. I should say the funniest group of people that mean to be funny. Canada's funniest group of people that don't mean to be funny are Albertans. See my various musings on Alberta and Albertans later in the book for more details.

The inherent humour and general good attitude that can be found in Newfoundlanders is also evidenced in the many odd community names that can be found in the province: Bacon Cove, Bareneed, Blow Me Down, Come By Chance, Conception Bay, Deadman's Bay, Goobies, Heart's Content, Jerry's Nose, Little Seldom, Nameless Cove, Sweet Bay, Tickle Cove, Witless Bay and many more.

There are, of course, some essential things that you should know about Newfoundland besides the funny stuff. The capital city is St. John's, and it is often mistaken for a city in New Brunswick called Saint John. They're not mixed up because they look alike but because they sound the same. So, as a fake Canadian, if you mix up these two cities it won't be that disastrous, unless you're talking to either a New Brunswicker or a Newfoundlander. So, remember, the capital of Newfoundland is St. John's and the capital of New Brunswick? Well, you'll have to wait for that until later in this chapter.

Newfoundland and Labrador is Canada's youngest province. It became part of Confederation in 1949. Prior to that, it was a British colony. Perhaps the fact that it was slow to join Canada is another reason that Canadians have made fun of Newfoundland. Or perhaps it's the unique accent that one person described to me as a speech impediment. Now, I wouldn't call a Newfie accent—that is, a Newfoundland accent—a speech impediment any more than I would try to describe to you what it sounds like. All I'll say is I've never heard anything quite like it, except maybe in the north of England.

Fishing has always been a big industry in Newfoundland. That's not a non sequitur, it's a fact—and it also gets me off the subject of accents. Anyway, other industries that have emerged are oil (on the ocean floor in an area called Hibernia), mining and forestry.

If you're wondering how to pronounce the name of this gem of a Canadian province, whose nickname is actually "The Rock," your guess is as good as mine. You will hear it pronounced as though it is three separate words as often as you will have the three run together. In central Canada, where I'm from, you will most often hear it pronounced Newf'ndland…I couldn't tell you whether that is right, wrong or Greek in origin.

The very last thing I think I'll write on the subject of Newfoundland is that it lays claim to having Canada's and North America's most easterly point, Cape Spear. Ouch!

The Maritimes

The Maritimes (or the Maritime Provinces) are different than the Atlantic Provinces. Newfoundland is excluded from this fine-feathered grouping. The Maritimes include Nova Scotia, Prince Edward Island and New Brunswick. It's a very exclusive club, don't ya know!

Nova Scotia

Nova Scotia lies on Canada's East Coast. Close by are the provinces of New Brunswick, which butts up against Nova Scotia on its western edge, and Prince Edward Island, which lies across the Northumberland Strait. Many people have described the shape of Nova Scotia as lobster-like and sticking out into the Atlantic. Personally, I don't see it, although I did once have a fine lobster dinner in the province.

Nova Scotia got its name from King James I of England. Translated from Latin, Nova Scotia means "New Scotland." Again, I don't see it, but who am I to judge? I mean, King James set people to work on creating the King James Version of the Bible. All I do is write these goofy little books. However, I have actually been to Nova Scotia. King James has not.

Tourist literature calls Nova Scotia "Canada's ocean playground." However, that is only true if you visit the province during summer. If you visit during winter, as I did, Nova Scotia is cold! And it's an incredibly damp and bone-chilling cold because of its ocean location. I spent a week there in December 1985, and it took me until 1995 to thaw out. Okay, I actually thawed out in 1994.

Tourism is one of the biggest industries in Nova Scotia, and why not? It is only second to the province of Québec in terms of historic sites. Some of those sights include the Halifax Citadel (that's a fort), the Fortress of Louisbourg (another fort) and Port Royal (a 17th century wooden fur-trading fort). The place has

more than a couple of forts, as you can see. There are also hundreds of sandy beaches and the almost mythical place known as Cape Breton Island. You should always refer to Cape Breton Island with reverence. I'm not exactly sure why, but that's what Canadians do. So, to fit in, do it.

Nova Scotia is also the legendary home of the Oak Island money pit. Oak Island lies in Mahone Bay on Nova Scotia's eastern shore. Since 1795, people have been trying to find out what's at the bottom of a big hole there. The search for stuff at the bottom of the pit and the deaths surrounding the search have been written up in books and have also suffered the ignominy of being examined in TV documentaries. So far, nothing's been found and nothing's conclusive, but people keep digging.

The largest city in Nova Scotia, and really the only one you have to remember, is Halifax. It is also the largest city in the Maritimes, and it is blessed with a deep, ice-free port year round. It is the home of Canada's Atlantic Fleet, which I think includes a broken submarine, a dinghy and a whistle. Okay, it's a bit bigger than that, but not much!

Halifax served as a major base of operations during both world wars. During World War I, it suffered the largest non-nuclear explosion ever recorded, when two ships collided in the harbour. Oops!

British general Edward Cornwallis originally founded the city in 1749. Americans may remember Cornwallis' nephew. He was a British General who fought against the Americans' secessionist action, or "Revolution" as it was called.

Across the harbour from Halifax lies Dartmouth. It used to be a city on its own, but it was amalgamated into Halifax during the heyday of Canadian city amalgamations in the 1990s. And there you have it. Nova Scotia wrapped up in a tidy little package—a cold and bone-chilling tidy little package, but a tidy little package nonetheless.

Prince Edward Island

Prince Edward Island is Canada's smallest province, both in terms of area and population. Its population, 138,000, is actually less than many minor cities in the rest of Canada. However, it is a full $\frac{1}{10}$ or $\frac{1}{13}$ partner in Confederation, depending on how you do your long and short division.

PEI is an island, as its name says, and up until 1997, it could only be reached by boat or airplane. Well, I guess you could have gotten there by swimming, too, or by helicopter. Let me just say that there was no bridge connecting it to the mainland. However, in 1997, the Confederation Bridge opened, linking PEI to New Brunswick. The island is separated from both Nova Scotia and New Brunswick by the Northumberland Strait, and now it's connected to New Brunswick by bridge. So, in theory, you can now walk to PEI from the rest of Canada or drive your car, or fly by airplane or get there in a number of other ways. But enough about transportation. Let's talk shapeliness. And PEI, well, she is damn shapely. At a mere 224 kilometres long, she's shaped like a jagged, inverted eyebrow. Just think about that! Oh, not the kind of shape you thought I was talking about? Stop being so cheeky!

PEI is best known for its red sand and for producing tons upon tons of spuds (that's potatoes to you Americans). It's also known as a major tourism destination for its fine beaches and for hauling out of the sea some tasty lobsters, oysters and Irish moss. Okay, the Irish moss may not be so tasty, but it is one of the many fishery products harvested on the island. That's because Irish moss contains a thickener called carrageenan. Anyways, the Prince Edward Islanders rake it in from where it grows not far from the shore. Then they send it off to be processed in some way that I'm not sure about (and neither are they). But it's a lovely cash crop for a sturdy and hearty people down east, don't ya know.

The other thing Prince Edward Island is known for is Anne of Green Gables, a character created by Lucy Maud Montgomery. Ever since Montgomery created her, the orphan girl has been foisted on Canada in the form of stories, books, plays and even movies and television. I have to be honest. I've never read the book, seen the entire movie(s) or watched the related TV crap. I tried to watch the TV show once, but my teeth began falling out because of the sugary sweetness of the material. As a Reasonable Facsimile of a Canadian, you should know about Anne, but luckily, the book isn't required reading. My apologies to all of those Islanders and Canadians of questionable taste who say they love Anne. I do not. I'm sorry, okay! Mostly for you.

The capital of Prince Edward Island is Charlottetown, the location where one of the pivotal meetings of Canada's Fathers of Confederation took place in 1864. The only other PEI locale you really need to remember is Summerside. That's because it's a place where a lot of official government paperwork gets sent—like income tax returns. I, for one, always fill out my income tax returns and send them in on time. Everyone should. It's very Canadian. Luv ya, Summerside!

New Brunswick

What can one really say about the last of the Maritime and Atlantic Provinces? What indeed? What? What? What? Well, it's the most westerly of Canada's easternmost provinces. That's a start. It's also one of the original four. The original four are, of course, the original four provinces that came together to be Canada: New Brunswick, Nova Scotia, Québec and Ontario (I'll move on to those last two next).

But let's get back to the subject of New Brunswick. The province is roughly rectangular; actually it's more like a parallelogram that drifts to the left at the top and to the right at the bottom. It's located on the east coast, although it is the only one of the three Maritime provinces that has any sort of land border with either the rest of Canada or the United states. Woohoo, there's a claim to fame. Ahem. It's actually sandwiched between the state of Maine on the southwest, the province of Québec on the northwest, the Bay of Fundy on the southeast and Nova Scotia, PEI and the Gulf of St. Lawrence on the northeast. New Brunswick is also connected to Nova Scotia by the Chignecto Isthmus. Try saying that three times fast! Chignecto Isthmus, Chignecto Isthmus, Chignecto Isthmus! Isn't that fun? I know the location all sounds a bit complicated, but if you look at a map, you'll get the idea.

The capital of New Brunswick is Fredericton, not Saint John or St. John's. St. John's, as you already know, is the capital of Newfoundland. Saint John is not a capital, but it is another city in the province of New Brunswick. Saint John is probably best known for its reversing falls—and being mixed up with the capital of Newfoundland. The falls at Saint John reverse direction because of ocean tidal forces. Moncton is another city in New Brunswick, and it is best known for the optical illusion known as Magnetic Hill, where cars appear to coast uphill. If you'd like to know more about either Moncton's Magnetic Hill or the reversing falls at Saint John, look it up on the internet or search for the very funny book, *Weird Canadian Places*, which contains an irreverent look at both of these oddities. I'm not sure who the author was on that book, though.

Now, let's hear more about the fascinating province of New Brunswick. It is Canada's only officially bilingual province, which means they speak two languages there. Anyone want to guess which two? Not Swahili and Urdu. Well, not officially anyways. The two official languages are English and French. And just why is that? Basically because the first inhabitants of what is now New Brunswick—after Native people, that is—were from France. They became known as Acadians, and many of them were expelled when the English took over the colony in 1755. Many of the Acadians were sent to the American colonies. A great many of them settled in what is now Louisiana, where they became that state's thriving Cajun population. Jambalaya anyone? Anyways, later on, some of the Acadians moved back to New Brunswick, and some others were able to hide from the British and were not expelled in the first place. This resulted in a large French-speaking population, thus the bilingual status of the province. There are some other reasons for bilingualism, but you needn't worry about them. Please don't ever say New Brunswickers are bilingual because they can't make up their minds. That certainly could not be true.

Like other parts of the Maritimes, New Brunswick gets its fair share of snow in the winter and fog at various times of the year. It also has a thriving fisheries industry and is known for its lobsters, molluscs and amazing Atlantic salmon. They even have annual festivals here celebrating all the attributes of the lowly mollusc. Isn't that grand!

One final thing Americans may know about New Brunswick: a little place called Campobello Island. In the not so distant past, depending on how you measure time, former U.S. president Franklin Delano Roosevelt had his summer home on the tiny New Brunswick island known as Campobello.

Snow, fog, molluscs, oddities and Campobello—that's New Brunswick in a nutshell! Which does not in any way imply that the people are nuts or live in shells. Again, I've said enough. New Brunswick, yeehaw!

Central Canada

Central Canada is made up of the two largest provinces, Ontario and Québec. At various times in their history, Ontario and Québec have been linked as one. In the West, they call Central Canada "the East," but they say it as though it is the dreaded Empire from the Star Wars movies. The Prime Minister is often looked upon as Darth Vader no matter whether he comes from the West, the East or Central Canada. That's probably because Canada's capital city, Ottawa—the seat of the evil Empire—lies within Central Canada. The Prime Minister is, however, rarely Darth Vader-like, unless he comes from the Conservative Party. That is, of course, my own little bias showing through there, not an out and out truth. Though it is pretty close to a reasonable facsimile of the truth.

The rest of the country often resents Central Canada because of the political clout wielded by the region. You see, most Canadians actually live in Central Canada—20 million of Canada's total 32.5 million. But people from elsewhere don't like the fact that because so many of us live here, we have a big say in what happens.

As Americans, you must know what it feels like to be the biggest and have "little 'uns" all over the place resenting you. Well, it's the same here in Canada. Of course, that doesn't mean that Canadians in Central Canada don't have some resentment towards the U.S. Because we do. And, our resentment and outrage is certainly justified much more than those who resent Central Canada. Or is it?

PRIME MINISTER STEPHEN HARPER

Québec

So what exactly do you need to know about the province of
Québec? Just about everything. Or at least you have to pretend
you know just about everything. Now I'm going to get into
trouble for thinking this, writing this and on occasion saying
this, but Québec really isn't happy unless it's the centre of attention. And the people of Québec just don't care how they get
that attention. Yep, in the family that is Canada, Québec is the
bratty little brother.

"Look at me! Look at me! I'm going to pout! I'm beautiful.
I remember. I never forget. I'm special. I'm different. I'm going
to run away!" Québec has said all of these things in some form
or another at some time or another. Well, the province is special, unique and interesting. It's also a pain in the ass! However,
most of the interesting people in the world, past, present and (dare
I say) future, have been royal pains in the ass. So why shouldn't it
be the same way with the most interesting parts of a country?

One only needs visit the province to realize how different it is
from the rest of Canada—how different it is than the rest of
North America. It's not just that it's an island of French adrift

in a sea of English. But for starters, that's pretty damn funny, if you dare think about it. It's also just a little bit sad, or on occasion scary, or even sometimes dangerous. But mostly Québec is one of the things that make Canada, Canada. Without Québec, the French language and the two founding peoples, Canada might as well be America, that is, the United States of America. And who wants that? I don't mean to offend, but if you're American and reading this book, you probably already agree. So onward I go.

Always remember that ongoing conflicts—like the conflict between English and French—make for a better story than just a bloody battle. A collective flipping of the bird at each other, behind our backs or directly, makes for an interesting, if not monumentally funny, country. Really! This collective bird flipping does more for keeping us together than any law, rule or forging in fire of battle. It's all about will and stamina. As in, "I'll keep annoying you, and I'll never give in." We stay together as much for sport as for spite. Now that's funny.

Conflict definitely equals funny. Don't take my word for it, look it up. I mean it, you lazy bastards, don't just sit there passively reading, look something up for yourselves. Or don't. Be all lazy about it.

Okay, finally back to Québec.

Québec is the largest province in Canada by area and the second largest by volume (or boast, as we like to call it). Not really. Volume and boasting are hard to quantify. Québec is the largest in terms of area and second largest in terms of population. It is the only province in which French is the lone official language. It's also the only province with a name requiring an accent over it's first 'e,' which means extra work for me every single time I write Québec. Again, it just goes to prove that the province is a pain in the ass. But I'm not giving into it—and I know it won't give in to me.

Québec (another accent) is actually quite similar to New York state. Not really. It's similar only because its capital city has the same name as the province, just like New York's largest city has the same name as the state. So, that makes Québec and New York almost identical, right? Not so right.

Québec got its name from an Algonkian word meaning "where the river narrows." That's because the location of the original Québec City is at a place on the St. Lawrence River where the river narrows. As you can see, the people of Québec (or at least its founders) were quite practical. Well, in some ways, anyway. In other ways, not so much. Again, I'll say it, that's what makes Québec, Québec.

Samuel de Champlain is considered the founder of Québec. In 1608, he founded Québec City, which is probably why they consider him Québec's founder, I mean, because he was. At least he was from a European perspective. We also know he had some help, but they don't say too much about his helpers.

The physical shape of the province of Québec is roughly like a right angle triangle with a big bite out of the angled side. So it's not really much like a triangle at all. There it goes being difficult again. The province is actually about three times the size of the place where its founding European people came from—that would be France. The province has more fresh water than any other Canadian division and it's covered by massive acres of forest. Forestry, energy, mining, fishing and tourism are the big industries in the province, along with sticking it to the rest of the country in a completely harmless, yet annoying bratty little brother way. The St. Lawrence River and Seaway, something that is shared with the United States, is the artery that runs through the province from the Gaspé Peninsula in the east to the Ontario border in the west.

As one of the founding four provinces—that's right, the bratty one was in on this experiment from the beginning—Québec has always held a special status. The word "special" can be interpreted in different ways depending on how you look at it. Well, that is Québec. It's all about how you look at it.

Québec's provincial flag is as different from the other provincial flags as Quebec's poutine is from French cooking. You see, the flag is blue and white and covered in fleurs de lis. Actually, just four, but they are big. The other provinces all have some form of red colour going on.

Back to poutine and French food—actually on second thought, I'll save that for the food section of your lessons. Look it up there, you'll love it. Suffice it to say, the Québecois food known as poutine does not resemble the refined recipes that one normally associates with the French.

Cities you should remember include, Québec City, which is the capital; Montreal, which is Québec's largest city; Trois Rivières; Shawinigan; Hull, which is across the Ottawa River from Ottawa; Rimouski; Sherbrooke; and Baie Comeau, where the reviled ex-Prime Minister Brian Mulroney comes from.

We love Québec and we hate her, and she feels the same way about the rest of us. But without Québec (yet another accent), we really wouldn't be half as interesting. And on those mornings when we're really bored and looking for something to do while having breakfast, we have the French side of the cereal box to read. That, my friends, is a very good thing. Je me souviens! Je me souviens libre!

Ontario

What can you say about a province that has the common loon as its bird symbol? Crazy, wacky, odd, disturbed or "what a mistake it was letting the kids pick the provincial bird?" The truth is that school kids ages 9–11 chose the loon as Ontario's bird symbol. I am sure that bureaucrats were fired and politicians ran screaming from the legislature when the kids' choice was announced. I've read part of the legislative debate over adopting the common loon as Ontario's bird symbol. Now if that debate wasn't wacky, I don't know what is. I guess politicians need wacky diversions like everyone else, and they had great fun back in 1989 talking this one through. Other birds, like the buzzard and yellow-bellied sapsucker, were mentioned during "The Great Loony Debate," as much for politicians to refer to their political opponents as anything. The debate was long, but the kids spoke, and the common loon won out. The child who wrote the winning essay supporting the common loon said the birds look funny when they walk—much like a politician

when he's telling the truth, I guess. Still the common loon was adopted as the bird symbol. I guess it's a better reason than "my uncle Marty has stock in common loons." Funny, though, school kids haven't been asked to name anything ever since, and uncle Marty dumped his common loon stock.

Other things you should know about Ontario? Well, it's the region I would suggest that you tell people you come from in your quest to be a Reasonable Facsimile of a Canadian. And just why is that? Well, Ontario's shaped like a pork chop, of course. And…the pork chop is the easiest…meat product…you can fake…looking…like you…come from? That doesn't make much sense. However, it is true that Ontario is shaped like a pork chop. Or at least a pork chop that Elvis Presley once had a bit of a gnaw on.

The province is sandwiched between Manitoba to the west and Québec to the east. It's also sandwiched between the Great Lakes in the south and Hudson Bay and James Bay in the north. As an aside and dealing with all of this sandwiching, a pork chop sandwich is always a nice choice for a leftover lunch. I mean as long as it's boneless. I think McDonald's found out the hard way that a bone-in pork sandwich isn't that appealing and can be slightly painful. That's why their McRib never caught on. Or that's my theory, anyway.

As I was saying, though, Ontario is definitely the region that you should pretend to come from if you are trying to pretend to be a Canadian. The short reason is because it's the largest province in Canada by population, making it easy to get lost in Ontario. There are many large cities that you can say you come from—Toronto, Hamilton. Ottawa, London, Niagara Falls, Windsor, North Bay, Sudbury, Timmins, Thunder Bay, Kenora, and the list goes on. Just pick up a map or do some research on the website for the city you want to pretend to come from, and you'll be swamped by facts, lore and uninteresting figures galore. The websites are not likely to be presented in as interesting or fun-filled ways as I lay things out for you, but they are more likely to be accurate and extol the great virtues of their fair communities. Woohoo Dundas!

Another reason you'd be wise to choose Ontario as your fake home is that the Ontario accent is probably the easiest for Americans to emulate. It most resembles that of TV sitcom characters. Some would say the Ontario accent is almost Midwestern in terms of comparing it to an American region. But really, just watch a few American sitcoms, and the Ontario accent comes through—as long as the sitcom isn't based in the South or New York. I mean no Ontarians or Canadians, let alone troubled peoples of the world, have that unfortunate New York accent. And the southern accent is wonderful, but we don't sound like that either. If you're an American with a thick southern or New York accent, I'd suggest you would be better off going into hiding than trying to be a fake Canadian. It just won't work.

Anyway, the Iroquoians—they were a Native Canadian group that inhabited the region before Europeans arrived—called Ontario "Kanadario," which means sparkling water. There was some sort of copyright dispute over future ownership of a sparkling water company, so the province dropped the Iroquoian "k," rearranged the letters slightly, added an "o" and there you have it: Ontario. A new province was born, and the Iroquois got screwed out of naming rights. Later they got back at us, though, by building casinos.

The Iroquoian name about the sparkling water, is however, appropriate. Ontario is covered in water—it's soggy from one end to the other. Well, not on the land, unless it rains, which it doesn't do that much, but nonetheless there is a lot of water here. One-sixth of the province is covered in it, and although that's a really nifty statistic—taken from the premier's own website—it's not going to help you much in being a Reasonable Facsimile of a Canadian. Just remember we've got lakes, we've got rivers, we've got bays, we've got canals, we've got waterfalls and we've even got wetlands, which doesn't mean that all of our land is wet. However, many of our politicians are. Wet, that is… or sweaty. Some of them are even slimy. Yep, Ontario is like all big jurisdictional places, full of pesky, sweaty, slimy, weasel-like politicians. But they are a separate set all unto their own, and aren't we all just grateful that we're not one of them. Unless you are one of them, and then, of course, I'm just kidding. (Following to be read in a monotone voice.) Oh yes. Really. Really. I am just kidding.

As I was saying, Ontario's got a lot of people to get lost among and an accent that's easy to get as well as a lot of big and small places to get lost in. It's the second largest province in terms of area, don't ya know. If I've repeated myself on this point, just keep reading. It'll be forgotten soon enough when another daz-zlingly amusing and informatively witty tidbit comes along.

"Loyal she began, and loyal she remains." Doesn't sound like a motto that would be adopted by this wacky place called Ontario, now does it? Or maybe it does. Anyways, that is, in fact the Ontario motto, which fits with the fact that Ontario was one of the original four provinces. It's also been the economic engine and the backbone of the country since Confederation. There's mining, manufacturing and even a couple of cartoon character fun factories here. There are steel mills and forestry—pulp, paper and lumber—farming and finance and a whole lot of peo-ple to serve you. Most people in the province work in some kind of service industry.

Ontario has a lot to offer, including the capital city of Canada, Ottawa; the largest city in Canada, Toronto (also the provincial capital); and a coat of arms with cute little animals on it— moose, deer and bear. Okay the animals on the coat of arms aren't so much cute as they are stiff, as if they don't like having their pictures taken and some guy's standing off camera threatening them with a shotgun—probably American singer

Ted Nugent, who likes to hunt here. You see, Ontario has everything and (sometimes) Ted Nugent, too!

The West

The four western provinces (Manitoba, Saskatchewan, Alberta and British Columbia—aka The West) are west of the eastern provinces. There is no trick here as with the Northwest Territories, though most of the western provinces at one time or another were part of the Northwest Territories. The West doesn't have as many lakes or rivers or water in general as the central provinces, although it does have some rather big lakes and rivers and even the Pacific Ocean—and that's no slouch. None of the western provinces are as big as Canada's biggest provinces and there aren't nearly as many people in the West as "Back East." However, the West has something the East does not—Portage La Prairie. What I mean by that is some odd French place names, big sky country and a long way to walk to the far end.

The name Portage La Prairie means "there are no rivers here and the land is real flat so we're going to have to carry the canoe for a bit, eh!" Well, it doesn't actually mean that, not literally, but it is located on the prairie and portage does mean "a place where the boats have to be carried." I added a bit of colour in my translation, but basically, it stands true—unless the good folks of the city of Portage La Prairie, population 20,000, have just used this as a clever ruse to attract people who like to carry their boats. But I think not.

What you should most know about the West is that people there don't much like being compared to the East. And when they say "the East" in the West, they mainly mean Ontario or sometimes all of Central Canada, including Québec. You can understand their desire to not be compared to the East—there really is no comparison. I think no matter how you look at my last statement, all sides can be proud. And that, my friends, is the essence of the West—they are proud people. They should be. They've got Portage La Prairie and other equally oddly named places like Climax, Head Smashed In Buffalo Jump and Pouce Coupe, which is French for "cut thumb." Pouce Coupe may also be a song by the American group, the Beach Boys.

The Prairies

The easternmost three of the western provinces are often referred to as the Prairies. That's because they have vast areas of land that are completely flat. If Columbus had lived on the Prairies, he would have thought the world was flat, the New World would never have been "discovered" by him and whole populations of indigenous peoples wouldn't have been wiped out by European conquerors and disease. But Columbus—the famous Christopher of 1492 fame that is—did not live on Canada's prairies. Well, there is no evidence of it anyway. So, the New World was "discovered," indigenous peoples were decimated and Canada's prairie provinces are here to stay. Physically anyway. It's anyone's guess as to whether they'll stay politically.

The Prairie Provinces are made up of Manitoba, Saskatchewan and Alberta, though Canada's prairie is really only located in the southern half of those provinces. The term "prairie" is actually French and describes a vast sea of flat, treeless grass like an Italian-Canadian's front lawn in the heart of Toronto. But the Prairies are not like an Italian-Canadian's front lawn in the heart of Toronto. For one thing the Prairies are not in the heart of Toronto, and well, I needn't go into the rest since I'll probably only get myself into trouble with Italian-Canadians, whom I love.

So, back to the Prairies. Although the name suggests flat grasslands with no trees, the Prairies have a lot more to offer. There is a lot of flat grassland with no trees, don't get me wrong, but in some places there are also little hills that they would call speed bumps in the East, or should I say evil or dreaded East? Kidding. I kid because I love!

The Prairies do have vast plains, but they also include picturesque plateaus, mystical valleys and lush rolling hills. It may seem like I padded the last sentence with over-the-top adjectives, but I didn't. That is really what I think of the Prairies.

The Prairie provinces, you Americans should know, are a beautiful place where some very fine people live, and you should visit them as often as you like or can. The Prairies, woohoo!

Manitoba

I was doing research one time and came across a "poem" that I think could be considered the song of Manitoba. It goes like this:

> *Manitoba, Manitoba,*
> *Just like Barcelona,*
> *But not!*
> *Manitoba, Manitoba*
> *What the hell is that?*
> *It's a deer fly, or a horse fly,*

It's a giant big black bug,
Oh my!
No it can't be, you're kidding me,
I think it wants a hug.
I'm wrong, how stupid,
It's opened a great big maw.
Big mouth!
Yikes and ouchy,
Oh merciful gawd uh—ahhhhh!
My feet are gone, my legs are gone,
Oh gawd, I'm a bloody stump!
Call me Matt.
Now it's turned on my car,
It's a mangled, smouldering clump!
Manitob…

And that's where the poem/Manitoba song ends. To say the least, the work is not of the calibre of say, someone like Bill Shakespeare. Though it does have the rather halting metre of someone like William Shatner. So, it's not a Shakespeare, but it could be a Bill. And that is something—though I'm not sure what. It also tells a keen little story and manages, in a very few lines, to engage us with some heartfelt emotion. It is missing an ending, although one is implied and/or truncated, perhaps for good reason. All in all, it is an awful little poem, though it could make a terrific rock ballad.

So why then have I included said awful little poem/terrific rock ballad in this section on the first of the western provinces? Well, it illustrates an aspect of Manitoba that you, as an Aspiring Reasonable Facsimile of a Canadian, ought to know about the province. It's got really big bugs. In the spring, especially if it's a wet spring, the bugs are even more plentiful, and they have been known to devour entire vehicles of 1970s vintage made by Buick. That's right, I'm talking big schooner-like vehicles eaten by large swarms of multi-legged, tentacle-laden buzzers.

So there you have it. Manitoba has big bugs. Winnipeg—Manitoba's capital city—has been called the mosquito capital of Canada. I know that doesn't sound like a great tourist draw, but entomologists have to vacation somewhere. So why not in Winnipeg? Winnipeg's other great draws are the fact that it is one of the flattest places on Earth; it claims to have the windiest, coldest intersection in Canada—Portage and Main—and it's in the middle of the country. That's right, it's squashed right in the centre. Although it does not act like a troubled middle child—it lets Calgary in Alberta do that. Just kidding, Alberta. (And you'll see, my dear readers.)

But why am I so foolishly wasting valuable space on a place that speaks for itself? Well, it doesn't really speak for itself, it just sounds like it does from the hum that results from millions upon millions of bugs descending on the city with flapping wings in summer, or the wail of the whistling winds in winter.

Manitoba is referred to as the "Keystone Province." Apparently this is true, although it's not really called that by too many people, so that fact is not that necessary for you to remember. Although, visually speaking, it might help you place the province geographically. A keystone, architecturally speaking, is the central stone that locks everything together. Without a keystone, an arch would break up into its component parts, and they would all fall in on one another. With the keystone, the arch stands firm. This is the metaphor used to describe the place Manitoba has in Canada—or else it might just mean that Manitoba is in the middle. You know, on final analysis, I think it does just mean it's in the middle, even though Manitoba is not considered part of Central Canada. It's part of the West. So then maybe on final final analysis, Manitoba is the province that holds Confederation together. Let's throw them a bone and say that's what they are. But keep it on the q.t. when it comes to Québec, because Québec certainly wouldn't feel entirely comfortable with this interpretation or the throwing of said bone in Manitoba's general direction.

For your Aspiring Reasonable Facsimile of a Canadian purposes, Manitoba's in the middle—smack-dab between Ontario and Saskatchewan and snuggled up to the American states of Minnesota and North Dakota in the south and dear, new Nunavut in the north. A large portion of the northeastern part also lies along the shores of Hudson Bay. Does it not sound like Manitoba has everything? And yet there's more.

Manitoba is roughly shaped like an arrow pointing northwest, where the right side of the arrow has been bitten off by a giant monster. It has a shape that defies simple geometrical description like Québec, and it doesn't resemble Elvis leftovers like Ontario. However, Manitoba does have something in common with Ontario besides a border. Its flag is similar to that of Ontario, except Manitoba's has a butch little buffalo on its crest. As for poofter Ontario, its crest has three little maple leaves. I wonder which would win out in a hypothetical fight, a buffalo or some maple leaves? No seriously, that's the kind of thing I wonder. Is it any surprise that I write these goofy little books? Not that this one is goofy. It's totally serious and meant to help out the less fortunate. (That's you.)

Manitoba was the fifth province to join Canada. You should probably know that, but please don't obsess over it. Originally, the province was quite small, but it has been expanded a couple of times—at the expense of the Northwest Territories. Won't that territory ever learn?

Unlike most of the other provinces, Manitoba has no motto. Its name is most likely derived from a Cree phrase meaning "God who speaks," or "Place where the spirit speaks," or even "What the hell is a Manitoba?" Okay, the last one is mine, but when they start saying things like "it most likely means," it's clear to me that they have absolutely no freakin' idea.

You should know, at least in passing, that wheat is a major cash crop in Manitoba and that the local winters are cold. You should also know that southern Manitoba has suffered several major floods over the years from the Red River, much like communities in North Dakota and Minnesota in the U.S.

The other cities and towns you should at least recognize in terms of names are Flin Flon because it's odd; Brandon, which is the 90210-inspired town (not really); and Churchill, where polar bears have been known to wander into town and well, call the shots. You should also know that Lake Winnipeg lies within the borders of Manitoba, and it's big. Lake Winnipeg also has a sister lake, named Lake Winnipegosis—the name, unfortunately, is no joke. It seems that the bureaucrats of Manitoba had used up all of their creative abilities when it came to naming Lake Winnipegosis. It could be that it was late on a Friday, and they thought, "Hey, just add -osis to Winnipeg and we can all knock off early!" I can't say I have confirmation on this interpretation, but it seems whomever named the lake was in coasting mode. But you didn't hear that from me.

Saskatchewan

Ah, the practical people of Saskatchewan. That is the main thing you should take away from this section. The folks there, and I dare say you can call the people of Saskatchewan folks, are nothing if not practical. And, I believe they are the people who bind this country together.

Whereas people in other parts of Canada regularly put their clocks forward in the spring and backward in the fall, in Saskatchewan, they'll have none of this nonsense. The concept, the idea even, of Daylight Savings Time is completely lost on these folks. Springing forward, falling back, an hour here, an hour there, just so we can get up earlier to catch the sun, makes no sense in Saskatchewan. If they need to get up an hour earlier to make the best use of the daylight hours, you'll never guess what those Saskatchewaners do. They get up an hour earlier. They don't need the government or the official time signal in Ottawa to tell them when to get up. They just do it. I can hear the laughter in Regina and Saskatoon and all the beautiful rural places that dot the province when each Daylight Savings Time rolls around and the rest of us rush around our houses like dingbats on acid changing our clocks to coincide with the new official time. In Saskatchewan, they stand back smoking their pipes, rocking in their rocking chairs and saying things like "There they go again, Martha," and "Yep." They shake their heads slowly and smile gently, for in Saskatchewan the time is always the same, which does not imply in any way, shape or form that Saskatchewan and her people are stuck in time.

IMPORTANT NOTE: My view of, interpretation of, and illustrative scenarios involving the people of Saskatchewan may not be entirely accurate. In fact, my picture of them may fall into the realm of stereotype. I apologize now to the good people of Saskatchewan if I have given a false impression of them. However, the picture of these people as I have painted it does illustrate a widely held view of Saskatchewan people, even if it is wrong. But remember, for your purposes as an Aspiring Reasonable Facsimile of a Canadian, holding an incorrect view that is widely held by the people you are trying to emulate will, in fact, allow you to fit in just fine. Again, to Saskatchewan, I apologize.

Saskatchewaners or Saskatchewanians—either term works for them—are the people that hold this country together. That's because they are a practical yet progressive people. People in all parts of Canada like to be known for two things: being progressive and being practical. However, many of us aren't always practical or progressive, especially in Saskatchewan's next-door neighbour, Alberta. I mean, those rednecks are nuts! Just kidding, Alberta.

Saskatchewan is the birthplace of universal medical care in Canada—or Communism, as most Americans would call it. But, let us try to forget what Americans might call it. Okay, forgotten.

As far back as 1962, this rectangular province was ensuring that its citizens were taken care of, medically speaking. If that's not

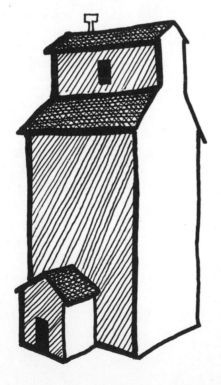

practical, then I don't know what is! They led the way on this issue in Canada. If that's not progressive then I don't know what is! In Saskatchewan, they seem to have the ability to collect all the good ideas that come through Canada, filter them in a progressive and timely manner and deliver them in the most practical and acceptable ways possible. I don't know why they have this talent. Perhaps it's their strong agricultural roots that continue to guide everything they do today. Perhaps they are just smarties of the highest order. I am, of course, not referring to candy-coated chocolate, but people of the highest intelligence here.

Saskatchewan is still the most rural of all Canada's provinces, and agriculture is its biggest industry. It produces more wheat than any other place in Canada and remains one of the top wheat producers in the world. The grain elevators that dot the prairie are a long-standing image of the province. Saskatchewan also cultivates a hefty crop of canola. Mining potash and uranium has become a big deal, and the province also has substantial natural gas reserves and even some petroleum. What potash is used for, I'm not really sure, and I didn't really want to do a lot of research on it. But I am sure it has nothing to do with marijuana, or "pot" as it is called colloquially.

Saskatchewan is the only province that has entirely artificial borders. Or so I've read. But aren't most borders artificial? Recent events might even suggest that borders are really there only for pushing back, ignoring, bending—or in the case of the U.S.–Mexico border, leaping over or crawling under the fence. Borders, however, aren't usually as rectangular as those of Saskatchewan, but that's what happens when you're landlocked, carved out of the former Northwest Territories and forced to become a province along with Alberta in 1905.

Long before 1905, humans inhabited the area now known as Saskatchewan. The province has seen humans as far back as 10,000 B.C. The original human inhabitants are dead now from disease, hunting accidents and even old age. But their collective spirits live on. The original humans in Saskatchewan were just tagging along with the bison herds. European trappers and explorers followed much later, and they were in turn followed by the Northwest Mounted Police. Yes, the venerable Mounties in their red tunics passed through on their great March West. Eventually, people stayed, and after a rebellion and a battle, the province was born—more or less.

Geographically speaking, you should know that Regina is the capital city, and Saskatoon is an important city as well. These are really the only two cities in Saskatchewan of any size. Regina is also known as the sunniest capital city in Canada. That's because the people of Regina always wear smiles on their faces since they are deranged. Kidding. It's because Regina sees the sunniest weather of any capital in Canada. I told you Saskatchewanians were practical, and I think we can add straightforward to that as well.

The province stole its name from the Saskatchewan River. Well, it didn't steal it, exactly. The river still has the same name. I guess I could more accurately say that the province copied its name from the river. And the river is quite annoyed about it. In Cree, saskatchewan loosely translates to "swiftly flowing river." And guess what? The Saskatchewan River—it flows swiftly. Are you getting the overwhelming idea behind Saskatchewan? Good, because I need to move on to Alberta. And man, is that province going to get an earful!

Alberta

Alberta is perhaps the one place in Canada that is perfect and pristine and embodies all that is holy. Its people are scholars, and its politicians are gems. Gems in the rough, as it were, for you will have to dig beneath the surface, through rugged, craggy, diamond-like hardness, to find the gem part, but I'm told the gems are there. The flora and the fauna of the province are pretty and friendly, respectively speaking, and the hunters pack a wallop with six shooters, semi-automatic rifles and old reliable shotguns. It's a lot like America, but without the right-wing religious zealots. Let me rephrase that. It's a lot like America.

Then there are the Stetson hats. You're not Albertan if you don't sport a Stetson hat in public at some point or another, in the same way that you're not really a British comedy actor unless

you dress up and portray a really ugly woman at some point in time. Of course, for the Brit actor, dressing up like a woman doesn't mean you're gay. So, for an Albertan, putting on a Stetson hat doesn't make you a real cowboy. As for the gay part, I would not like to speculate on that. Actually I would, but I won't.

I started out this Alberta section by trying to smooth over some of the feathers that I may have ruffled when it comes to what I have said about Alberta. I had intended and even started to be nice and congenial in speaking about Alberta and Albertans, knowing full well that some of them will read this book. But I cannot, I must not and I will not veer from the task at hand: to give you—the most desperate of Americans who want to pretend to be

Canadian—the most comprehensive, truthful and unbiased account (okay, maybe a little biased) of what you should know, think or do about your adopted homeland. So because of that, I am going to have to tell the truth about Alberta.

In actuality, I don't think that much about Alberta, and perhaps that is what pisses Albertans off. Not that I personally don't think much about it, but that Canadians in general don't think much about it. Because that is the essence of Alberta and Albertans—they're Canada's Pissed-Off People. Oh, dear, this is going badly. Perhaps I should stick to the geographical aspects of Alberta.

Alberta is shaped a lot like Saskatchewan, except in its left rear fender, where it looks like it's been dinged in an automobile accident. The accident in this case was butting up against the Rocky Mountains. I suspect that if the Rocky Mountains butted up against you, your car and/or province would be a write-off and you'd be better off hauling the whole thing to a junk dealer and starting over again from scratch. I do not recommend this for Alberta. But look, the Rockies have dented Alberta's fender and driven off leaving it a mangled mess for good. Perhaps what I should say is that the Rocky Mountains form a natural border in the southwest corner of Alberta where it meets up with British Columbia. Much nicer, no?

Come on, Alberta, you can accept that as a compliment, right? I'm hearing crickets chirping. All right, if they're going to be that way about it. Let me continue.

Alberta has many of the same features as its sister prairie provinces—you know, flatlands, wheat and all that tourist-drawing…stuff. So, I needn't go into that. It also has foothills, which aren't quite mountains, and the whole nature thing is really lost on me. I remember thinking as a kid that it would be amazing to see the Rocky Mountains. Then, as an adult, I saw them. And then, five minutes later, I was saying, "So now what?

Do they do anything else? Is there a dinner show? Laser lights? Anything?" But no.

I saw the mountains in British Columbia before I saw the mountains in Alberta, so maybe the whole mountain experience was ruined for me because they're bigger and more plentiful in BC, not just because mountains don't do anything. I don't know. Hey, maybe that's not it, but maybe it's a symptom. You see, when we think of mountains in Canada, we think of British Columbia. Alberta has them, but naturally, we just think of BC. When we think of vast prairies in Canada, we think of Saskatchewan, even though Alberta grows tons and tons of wheat. When we think of money and power, we think of Ontario. When we think "way out west," we think of BC again—both because they're wacky there and because they are located farthest west. No matter what Canadian thing we think of, even if Alberta has it, we think of some other place, region or even tiny shack as possessing it. Perhaps that is what's pissing off Albertans? Alberta, no matter what, seems to get shunted aside as not being the quintessential anything in Canada. Wow! That's something to ponder now, isn't it?

Hmmm…mmmmhmmmm…

That's got to make Alberta feel a bit better. I mean, look how long we all pondered her. How she's not thought of as quintessentially anything in terms of Canada. But while I was pondering, I thought of something. That's often what happens to me when I ponder. This is what I came up with, and I am sorry if I repeat myself again, but it doesn't work unless I do.

Alberta isn't thought of as quintessentially anything in terms of Canada, unless we're talking oil. When we think of oil in Canada (when we aren't thinking about high gasoline prices and are actually thinking about where there is oil in Canada), we think of Alberta. Sometimes we think of Newfoundland, but no, mainly we think of Alberta when it comes to oil. Although the first oil well in the country was actually in Ontario. But let's forget that. Let's say we think of oil with Alberta. Oil naturally means money and wealth and material things, which Alberta is happy and glad and ecstatic to tell us they have: "No sales tax, the lowest income tax in the country and government surpluses so large they send the people of the province rebate cheques!" That is quintessentially Alberta—new money, wealth and great new things because, wow man, look at all this oil out here and look at the price of it on the world market. Windfall!

Are you now seeing the problem that attitude causes? That falls into the category of showing off, which, as I explained in Chapter One, is something that Canadians don't like and don't do. One of our own doing it, we like even less. So we ignore them because we are embarrassed for them. We could also be a bit jealous or envious. Let's face it; Canadians aren't saints.

But let's get back to Alberta showing off. They drive to the store and then tell us how much they spent and how there was no

tax and how they've got the biggest, the loudest and the best of absolutely everything. So then we begin to wonder. If it is the biggest, the loudest and the best, why are you so desperate to convince us that it is so? Perhaps, despite all the money you spent, it's not. So then it becomes a bit of a game. Alberta keeps bragging louder and louder, and we ignore it more and more, because people that keep talking about money become rather boorish.

Then they develop a splinter political party. Yawn. Or at least that's what they see, because by this point it's easy to rile them, and it's become really fun—sport even. It becomes fun to see how the braggart who says he has the biggest, the loudest and the best suddenly becomes huffy because the money may have bought him stuff, but it hasn't bought him what he wants most—attention. And it never will. Alberta is a wonderful middle child who just needs to accept it, be it and not ever feel the need to prove its worth.

Now there are a few other things you should remember about Alberta and Albertans in your quest for status as a Reasonable Facsimile of Canadian. Calgary is the largest city and the place where most of the money can be found in the province. Apparently, they're just giving it away there. Sorry, they're not actually giving it away, but they will definitely sell it to you. Calgary is pretty much the western business capital, which means it's a smaller version of Toronto. And no, I didn't mean anything by the "smaller" remark, okay Calgary? Calgary has some very tall buildings, which means it's a lot like Dallas or Denver to you, my American friends.

On to Edmonton. Edmonton is the provincial capital, and the people there are a little more like the rest of Canada. I know a number of people who live or are from there, and they are much less interested in proving their size, volume or wealth than in getting down to the nitty-gritty of everyday living. Which does not make them better than Calgarians in any way, shape or form.

Another Alberta community name you should recognize, if not remember, is Fort McMurray, which sounds a lot like Fred McMurray, who played the father on that TV show, *My Three Sons* (which incidentally had more than three sons, but that's TV for you). Then there are Banff and Jasper. They weren't on *My Three Sons*, but they are in Alberta. They are small—I think they are okay with being called small—Rocky Mountain communities basically set up for tourists to visit and gasp: "My God, it's beautiful here!" I've been to Banff, and yes, it is beautiful, as much as tacky tourist destinations can be beautiful. I did not gasp upon seeing the mountains; however, I did say "My God!" in reference to the cost of the hotel, which could only be described as very expensive. For your purposes, just say that you've been to one or the other and "Oh, it was beautiful!" The only other Alberta place you really need to remember is Medicine Hat, mainly because it's a funny name that I think means "We passed the hat around to pay for the medicine, but the rich Albertans didn't put anything in it." Kidding again, Albertans. Just kidding.

Albertans, as a people, are just a hoot and a half to have fun with—or make fun of, as you may have noticed. I expect the same from them in return. Albertans will on occasion actually hoot and sometimes say "a half." Usually it's "a half empty" as opposed to "a half full," but I think I've made my point on that. Albertans are also not afraid to do a whole mess of things to make a buck. They've got a huge Easter egg in one town, a load of dinosaur bones in the badlands and an official UFO landing pad in St. Paul. They've also got quite a sense of humour about all of these things and Canada too.

One of the biggest mistakes that Canadians make about Alberta is the origin of her name. We all think she was named after Queen Victoria's husband, Prince Albert. But she wasn't. I'm not going to tell you who she was named after, since as wannabe Canadians you should make the same mistakes as us. Keep thinking Alberta was named after Prince Albert Saxe-Coburg-Gotha. Then try making that full name roll off your tongue in a moment of passion. Hot!

Albertans aren't just oil and bitterness, you should make sure to remember. Also remember they have both in large quantities and would be willing to sell them to you if the price is right. Yee haw!

British Columbia

British Columbia is neither British nor Colombian, though similarly to Colombia, some really good marijuana is grown there. Unlike Colombia, violent drug cartels do not control the province. However, some stubborn unions have virtually shut down the place at various times during its history. Really, when Canadians think of British Columbia, we think of tall trees, salmon and striking unionists. BC has all three in abundance, and for your purposes, you should never forget it.

British Columbia is more often referred to by its initials, BC. Why? Because it's shorter. BC's people have also elected some wacky people to run the place, which has given the rest of us the impression that British Columbians are just a little off kilter. We attribute this to the fact that they often say they can "swim in the morning and ski in the afternoon…and do it again the next day if they call a strike." Okay, the strike part isn't something they say, it's really just a given. Again, I kid, but you get my point, right?

They do often talk about being able to swim and ski in a single day, not because they can't commit to just one activity, but because they have a temperate climate on the Pacific Ocean, which allows them to swim, and they are surrounded by large snow-capped mountains, which allows them to ski. They apparently forget that skiing can also be done on water, so the rest of us can partake of similar activities in the same time frame. However, I think my point is slightly moot. They and they alone have an ocean to swim in and snow to ski on. Although there must also be places where one can ski on snow and swim in an indoor pool that is nearby. But a pool is not an ocean, although an ocean could be a pool for whales. Again though, that doesn't really nullify what they say about swimming and skiing in BC.

All of this talk about swimming and skiing in BC may give you the impression that British Columbians are all about play, which is not true. However, they are more about play than other parts of the country. That's why so many people from other parts of the country move there. Lazy bastards! I mean, good for them!

The province actually gets its name from the Columbia River, which runs through it, although the Columbia River got its name from an American explorer named Robert Gray. He named the river after his ship *Columbia*. And so, British Columbians having a more playful, less concerned attitude about accuracy than the rest of us, said, "A name? A name? Huh-huh. That's hard. Hey, Columbia's a good name. There, we're done. Pass the dube, will ya, bud?" The British part of British Columbia comes from the fact that the province was originally a British colony and remained staunchly British in makeup until at least the 1950s. That, of course, meant the food in the province was bad, and the toothy grins were mighty crooked.

That all changed when people from other parts of Canada and Asia began moving to BC. Spices were imported, the food became tastier, and miraculously, the teeth all seemed to fall into place. Before that all occurred, though, BC saw some hard times, not the least of which was being ripped off by the United States and sold down the river by mother England. Perhaps that's when the toothy grins actually changed.

What I'm talking about is, of course, the Alaska Boundary Dispute. I gave all the words of the dispute a beginning capital letter to help emphasize how important an event it was. It could only be more important if I had capitalized every letter in each word…or, I suppose, if I had simply written that this was the most important incident in Canadian history. I didn't write that because the dispute was not the most important event in Canadian history, although it was big. The issue really came to a head when the United States purchased Alaska from Russia. They didn't underbid us or anything. We overspent on Rupert's Land (the Northwest Territories), so we didn't put in a bid because we were cash poor, or some such thing.

The dispute over the Alaska panhandle and its boundaries had been a long-standing issue; however, as good friends living in close proximity, the U.S. and Canada decided to settle the dispute through an international tribunal. The U.S. clearly stacked the deck in the tribunal. I'm not going to go into the details, because it's much easier to prove my point if I gloss over them. Let me put it this way, though. Three Americans and two Canadians on the tribunal—you do the long division. Okay, there was also a British member who became the final tribunal panellist, but what help was that to us? The Merry Six—as I've taken to calling them—got down to business, as panellists will. They played "Password," "Match Game" and "What's My Line," as panellists do, and the British guy became wealthy in an unexplained and suspicious manner. In the end—surprise, surprise—the U.S. won the dispute. Okay, I can't prove that they played "Password" or that the British guy got rich in a suspicious manner, but I think it's clearly implied. Anyway, the United States won the dispute, and the boundary line was drawn in their favour on all but some minor islands they threw Canada's way. The Canadians on the tribunal panel refused to sign the resolution, stopping just short of saying the fix was in. Again, it was clearly implied.

Soon after, in all parts of Canada, violent anti-British sentiments erupted…into quiet, understated demonstrations.
Dentists were called and wooed, and everyone in Canada had
their teeth straightened in protest. We weren't too happy with
the Americans at that point either, so we farted en masse.
Great, smelly tornadoes formed over the Midwest and have been
"reeking" havoc ever since. We did eventually get over it, mostly
because the whole thing taught us two really good lessons—we
couldn't count on Britain, and we had to be wary of the United
States. Those sentiments have become a guiding principle
throughout our existence as a country.

If we have a dispute with the United States—whether it is over
boundaries, lumber or even joining a war effort in Iraq that had
absolutely nothing to do with 9-11—we know that if we don't
go along with the Americans they are somehow going to get us
for it. So, most of the time we go along. Sometimes we quietly
pretend we didn't hear what was asked. Sometimes that works.
But mostly, it doesn't. We know that America is for liberty and
freedom, zis-boom-bah, and that it likes us being its friendly
neighbour to the north. We also know that the U.S. only likes
all this and our being a separate democracy as long our democracy kowtows to theirs. Otherwise, the long knives come out,
and they send Tucker Carlson and Ann Coulter to attack us. And
let's face it, those rabid dogs are nuts. I say that with the utmost
respect for rabid dogs.

The Alaska Boundary Dispute helped forge the bonds of
Canada as a nation as much as the Revolution and Civil War
did for America. Many Canadians don't know much about the
Alaska Boundary Dispute. But what they do know is that
America won, it was unfair and we need to hold our cards close
to our vest. This has had long repercussions and spills over into
the political arena. We don't like our politicians to be outwardly
belligerent to America, because quite frankly, it's stupid, if not
impolite. However, even worse than a politician who is belligerent to the United States is one who is too cozy with and/or tries

to emulate an American president. Our current Prime minister, Stephen Harper, appears to be a lapdog to President George Bush. This will, at least in the long run, be his undoing.

All this we learned as a result of British Columbia joining the Canadian family. We also learned that the air on the western side of the Rockies is different from that on the eastern side, and when it is mixed with some BC homegrown it makes for a wacky yet cool place.

British Columbia is our westernmost province. It was the sixth to join the Canadian Confederation, which of course meant evenly matched partners when we had the annual barn dance. They've become the swingingest province in the country and aren't much up for barn dancing anymore, although they will go in for a whole lot of other freaky stuff!

The largest city in BC is Vancouver, which is also the third largest city in Canada. Vancouver is also a huge movie-making centre where hundreds of American movie and TV shows are filmed. If you're watching a TV show and it seems as though it's raining or cloudy a whole lot in the show, it was probably filmed in Vancouver…or the director meant for a it to have a rugged, moody, depressing aura to emphasize the emptiness of the human race despite the film being called *Blonde Co-eds 2: Those Girls Are Hotties!*

The capital of British Columbia is on Vancouver Island and is called Victoria after that famous British monarch of the same name. The city is also a place where a lot of old people live. In fact, it's been said that Victoria is where old Canadians go to die—or smoke some cheap homegrown so they won't care if they die. Either way, if you drive in Victoria, you should watch out for big cars that are being driven by little old men in hats who can't see over the steering wheels. On second thought, you should just walk while you're in Victoria—but still watch out for those old men and their big cars. Also have high tea at the Empress Hotel. It's what we're all supposed to do in Victoria… before we die there, that is.

CHAPTER FIVE

CANADIAN HISTORY, EH!

If one had to know Canadian history in order to be a Canadian, I'd be the only Canadian.

–Pierre Berton (1920–2004), Canadian Historian, Author and TV Personality, from *The Big Book of What We Think They'd Probably Say, or Perhaps Not*

Fakin' Your Way Through History Class

If there's one thing that Canadians know, it's their own history. Actually it's more like if there's one thing that Canadians really don't want to know, it's their own history. For you, as Aspiring Reasonable Facsimiles of Canadians, that simple fact bodes well. Once again, it means that you won't have to do a whole lot of studying or worrying about what you should know about Canadian history in order to pass yourself off as one of us.

Here's an example from my own life that should reassure you about your knowledge of Canada's history. While I was working on the Canadian version of *Who Wants To Be A Millionaire?*, the pronouncement came down from on high—that's the Ivory Tower, a.k.a. the second floor offices of CTV—that we should ensure the content of the show was 50 percent Canadian. This was unprecedented in terms of TV shows I had worked on before. It also became a ridiculous fantasy as things turned out. With the 50 percent Canadian content rule firmly clenched between our cheeks, we went about writing our nifty *Millionaire* questions. One day, a producer came to me and said that she didn't like how the questions were shaping up. She and her friends didn't know anything about Canadian history. They were much more interested in pop culture. "Ya know, like who was Jennifer Aniston dating?" She wasn't embarrassed by her lack of knowledge about Canada or by the fact that she and her friends were clearly idiots. Now, she is not a typical Canadian in terms of wearing her lack of knowledge of Canada on her sleeve and admitting that the most interesting things to her and her friends were banal, although she is typical of TV producers, who are, as a lot, idiots. Okay, I may have overstated that. I have mostly known only Canadian TV producers, and they, as a group, are indeed idiots. I don't know about TV producers in other countries.

The point you should take from my example is that most Canadians are quiet about their knowledge of Canadian history because they, like the idiot TV producer from my painfully true story, don't know that much. In fact, Canadians are likely to know more about American history than that of their own country. It's not because we're taught more American history in our schools than Canadian history. It's mainly because those of us who grew up at the tale end of the baby boom were fed a staple of American-made Warner Brothers cartoons. That's right, and I can safely say that Canadians picked up most of the history they know from Bugs Bunny. Bugs Bunny was highly entertaining, but he also managed to get the gist of history correct, if not all the details. Canadian history is often taught in a way that emphasizes details and dates instead of the greater scheme of things. Bugs Bunny, I can also safely say, is generally a better source of historical information than most other forms of televised history. That is the fault of TV producers and TV executives.

If you think I have been harsh in my assessment of TV producers you may want to know what I think of TV executives. They are the ones who ensure that the **Most Powerful Medium in the World** (my emphasis) has been squandered. That's because they are the biggest cowards in the world, always running scared and making decisions based on their fear. That's why Canada's Comedy Network is rarely funny, and Canadian TV drama is laughable.

The point of all of this historical set-up wrapped up in my assessment of TV is that you don't need to know that much about Canada and its history. You are rarely going to be asked questions about it, and if the subject ever comes up, just stay quiet. Everyone will assume you are typically Canadian in your lack of Canadian history knowledge, and the conversation will probably soon return to Jennifer Aniston, hockey or beer. For those of you who are still interested in learning a little about the place you're going to fake calling your own, here goes...

To Those Who Were Here First, We Salute You, eh!

Although you may often hear that the Native peoples—those we call the First Nations—were the first to live in Canada, it's not true. Long before they stumbled across the land bridge from Siberia following snowy rabbits or bison or their mommies, there had already been hundreds or millions or possibly billions and billions of inhabitants of Canada. Canada, you see, was as familiar with the primordial ooze as anywhere else on the vast planet we call Earth or home or terra firma. Of course, the ooze was not a life form as we know it, but what sprang from it was. So one can safely say that the First Nations were not first in Canada, but Ooze Springers were.

Then you've got your microscopic, single-cell, aquatic organisms that must have had some prescience (that means foreknowledge) when it came to what was to happen once Europeans arrived, for they were always going incognito by constantly changing their shapes. Harder for people to find you, categorize you and then off you that way, I guess. These single-cell life forms appeared long before the single-cell life forms we now refer to as politicians or lawyers.

The single cells begat more complex forms of life, and then fish and other bizarre aquatic creatures emerged, although Canada didn't produce an Olympic medal–winning swimmer until the 20th century. That's really more because we chose not to compete than because we weren't good enough. For Canada had its share of really fine, if large and hard to fit with a bathing suit, swimmers.

The misnamed, misunderstood and rather large group known as dinosaurs followed sometime later. Talk about your bulls in a china shop! In fact, each one was so much like a bull in a china shop that the Chinese refused to set up shop here at all. Scientists—archaeologist, palaeontologists and their ilk— suggest there were no china shops or even Chinese at the time because dinosaurs had the run of the land and the Chinese, as modern humans, didn't exist yet. But I do remember that fine film, *One Million Years B.C.*, where humans and dinosaurs co-existed. Humans who looked a lot like Racquel Welch existed right alongside dinosaurs. The scientists have suggested they need better proof than a film—things like fossil records or file cabinets full of alphabetized and detailed written records. But I ask you, who's being ridiculous now? We all know that the file cabinet is a 19th century invention…or at least you do now, and scientists as an educated group should already know it.

KLEINOSAURUS

If there is no record—written or fossil—of the co-existence of dinosaurs and humans, it's probably more because the dinosaurs were pigs when it came to eating and devoured everything in sight, including the earliest human-Canadians, which they called hors d'oeuvres. Although in dinosaur language, it was pronounced, "Err aaaaaaaaaaaaaaaahhhhhhhh. Gulp, gurgle, burp, pardon me!"

As for written records, well, they had no paper, no pens, and as I said earlier, no file cabinets. Let's face it, humans had to do a whole lot of hiding to keep from being lunch, and they certainly didn't want to create a paper trail that could give them away to the dinosaurs, or even worse, the income tax department.

So, in terms of what is acceptable as proof, I have no proof that humans co-existed in Canada alongside dinosaurs. Of course, we have more than a little proof that dinosaurs existed here. It's very difficult to hide a body of the size of an Albertosaurus... though I understand Ralph Klein is trying to lose weight. Isn't it also interesting that dinosaurs and Alberta go hand in hand in the same way that Conservatives and rednecks do? I have no idea what that means, except to say no matter where you stumble across Alberta's badlands, you can't help but run into dinosaurs and Conservatives. The dinosaurs have clearly passed on. Conservatives? Well, we'll see.

So, as much as I'd like to say that the First Nations were here first, well, the evidence does not bear that out, although bears have been known to be quite wily themselves and may have erased that evidence because of their inherent jealousy. So don't count out the First Nations yet!

And There Went the Neighbourhood, eh!

Canada was a quiet, peaceful and law-abiding place until the first modern humans arrived. Okay, it wasn't exactly law-abiding since there really weren't any laws except the survival of the fittest, which I guess made it a lot like the modern-day United States—without the right-wing religious zealots. I keep coming back to those zealots, don't I? Oh well.

The first humans arrived in Canada sometime between 25,000 and 50,000 BC Their estimated time of arrival in Canada makes scientists almost as reliable in terms of their pinpoint accuracy as Air Canada. Clearly, the term "around about" has some real history to it when it comes to Canada. You might want to make note of that.

The first humans arrived via the land bridge that connected Siberia to North America. There was a lot more ice in the world then, so few people went without cold drinks when there was a party, and of course the sea levels were lower, and land bridges popped up just about everywhere. People didn't race or float or fly their way into Canada, they just kind of walked from Siberia to Alaska and then south, not knowing exactly where they were going or why.

Gundar the *Homo Sapiens Sapiens* hunter probably mused, "So, I wonder where this path leads?" His friend Dundar most probably replied, "Unh? Wanna see?" And as they say, the rest is history. Some theories would suggest that Gundar and Dundar followed bison or mammoth herds across the bridge, since they weren't deep thinkers, natural leaders or at all curious, but I think my scenario is more likely. They came here, I believe, more out of boredom than anything. Their great excitement before that point had been realizing that their names sounded the same. On occasion, they also probably got themselves confused with one another.

Despite that, Gundar, Dundar and a whole host of others took those first tentative steps across the land bridge. Their first steps were tentative mainly because its edges were naturally quite icy, and *Homo Sapiens Sapiens* was afraid he might slip and chip a tooth, since modern dentistry hadn't been invented yet. In fact, dentistry of any scientific kind hadn't been invented, although people of the time were quite envious of the tusks of woolly mammoths—oh, and their wool because it was cold.

Soon after they crossed the land bridge—well not soon in terms of the length of a lifetime of a human, but soon in terms of world epochs—humans populated Canada. Okay, it was sparsely populated, but populated nonetheless.

We call the people that settled in Canada first the First Nations people. Actually, some of the original settlers were killed off by others who crossed later from Asia or by rival tribes that developed. So not all of those people that lived here were really here first, although we do still call them the First Nations. That's because they were here before the Europeans.

The First Nations happily got along in Canada for thousands of years. When I write that they happily got along, I don't mean Canada was a place without strife, rivalry, jealousy, war, famine or military takeover. The First Nations had all these fine things that modern cultures develop. They just did it in their own way and were happy to live as hunter-gatherers thriving in a Stone Age culture. Writing that the First Nations thrived within a Stone Age culture is in no way putting them down either. Stone tools are quite effective and take an immense amount of skill to produce. They are also extremely sharp, can do quite a lot of damage to human flesh and are also quite effective in killing animals. However, if you can drive herds of bison off cliffs to make them your lunch, then you don't lose any of your finely produced stone weapons, and you really don't need to invent the gun or gunpowder, do you? Thus, you are very happy to thrive in a Stone Age culture.

The First Nations were also effective, even fierce, warriors. The various tribes and nations often fought one another, and entire groups of peoples disappeared, were enslaved or became assimilated. Again, it's an example of how far the First Nations had come in terms of creating modern culture. The Inuit, for example, were not the first people to settle in Canada's Arctic regions. The original inhabitants weren't that good at living in the Arctic and were either killed off or pushed out by the Inuit.

We used to call the Inuit "Eskimos," which was an Algonkian term meaning "eaters of raw meat." The Inuit don't like that description, so we now call them by the name that they call themselves—Inuit. In their language, Inuktitut, Inuit means "the people." So, "the people" lived in "the Arctic" and did "the hunting," "the trapping" and "the kayaking."

They were also thriving quite well in Canada, as were the rest of the First Nations people, except for those who had been pushed out, killed off in conflict or had fallen in bison dung and couldn't get out.

…Then the Eurotrash Arrived, Eh!

Europeans, in the form of Norsemen, or Vikings, hit the shores and the balmy beaches of eastern Canada sometime around about the year AD 1000, and there went the neighbourhood. Well, actually, the first Europeans didn't take that well to Canada, I think more because they were homesick than anything. They did land and set-up communities, helmet and horn shops and corner herring stores. The Norse saw some sporadic success over about 300 years. They even traded with some of the First Nations, including the Inuit. The Inuit didn't much care for Viking "specials" on dried herring. The Vikings always seemed just a little too eager to push the herring, and the Inuit didn't much encourage the whole Eurotrash invasion in general. So eventually, the bottom fell out of the herring store market,

the helmet and horn stores collapsed and the Vikings left to plunder another place on another day. They did leave behind some nifty remnants of themselves in the form of artifacts and even decaying communities like L'Anse aux Meadows in Newfoundland.

That wasn't the end of the Europeans

But I'm sure you knew that. Columbus sailed the ocean blue in 14 hundred and 92—that's the year 1492 for those of you that are challenged lyrically, historically or numerically. The Portuguese were the unequivocal masters of the oceans and were making a tidy profit thanks to their spice trade. They were also a salty and fun-loving bunch that thought they'd mess with Columbus, who was always hanging around, eavesdropping and claiming he only spoke Italian. What Columbus didn't know was that the Portuguese had been fishing for cod off the Grand Banks (east of Newfoundland) for decades, if not a hundred years. They probably had even made contact with Canada's First Nations. With this knowledge in hand, they thought they'd rid themselves of Columbus once and for all. They let a little inside info slip out so that the impulsive Columbus would head off willy-nilly into the Atlantic and drown while trying to make his mark on the world. You see, the Portuguese knew that Columbus was always looking for an angle and was much more a shameless self-promoter than a good sailor. So the Portuguese gave Columbus the ammunition to shoot himself in the foot, or enough rope to hang himself, or at least a vast ocean to cross without swimming lessons or any great ability to navigate.

But then Columbus somehow managed to convince the Spanish to back him. Next thing you knew, he had ships and enough money to pay some real sailors. Then, of course, he smashed smack-dab into the Caribbean. Columbus returned to Europe, the cat was out of the bag and the Portuguese were left wondering what happened, or more accurately, *o que aconteceu?* So now that the floodgates of European expansion, exploration and discovery were wide open, well, the Europeans sailed in, and the idea of an all-Portuguese Canada kind of floated away.

Now the Americas were wide open to any Tom, Dick or Giovanni that came along…and come along he did, in the person of Giovanni Caboto, an Italian who couldn't convince the Italians to back him. He went against the family, hooked up with the British and discovered Newfoundland in 1497. The newly named John Cabot, as the British called him, was as dim-witted as Columbus. Cabot was searching for and was sure he'd find a northern route to the Orient. It was all about the Orient and spices at the time, and if you've ever tasted traditional English food, you can certainly understand their desperation. The search for a northern route to the spice trade is what pushed the exploration of Canada forward for some time, despite the fact that it was a major boondoggle.

And Then Came the French, Eh!

It wasn't until the mid 1530s that the French, in the guise of Jacques Cartier, discovered the mighty St. Lawrence River that led into the heart of what they slowly began to realize was a continent. Cartier also got naming rights to the northern country, which you wish to fake calling your home. In fact, the naming rights could be better described as misnaming rights. In 1535, Cartier was invited into a small grouping of First Nations dwellings. The natives referred to groupings of huts or individual villages by the term *Kanata*. Cartier thought the natives were referring to all the land and were inviting him to take it as plunder. Actually, he thought they had been referring to the entire country or even the continent as Kanata. The chance to plunder he saw as his God-given right. So, he and those that followed took to plundering the land that he and they now mistakenly referred to as Canada. The First Nations just stared on in disbelief and shook their collective heads with dismay.

The French were the ones responsible for opening up the continent, especially its northern environs. They did so mostly through business dealings—fishing, fur trading and looking for gold—and they did it with reckless abandon, as people with dollar signs in their eyes will. The First Nations people were becoming increasingly wary of these newest arrivals, and they began to get a bit snarky about it. In 1600, the French established the first European trading post in Canada around the nipples or near some breasts. That's right, Tadoussac, the location of the first trading post, translates from the native Mantagnais language as "nipples" or "breasts." Seems there were some rounded hills nearby that reminded the Mantagnais of breasts, and that's how the place got its name. Now that's a part of Canada you don't often see on tourism commercials, eh? Except the really dirty, late night, underground commercials that aren't sanctioned by any government—unless it gets you to visit, eh?

Champagne *Non*, But Champlain *Oui*, Eh!

The guy who really got the ball rolling in terms of colonization was Samuel de Champlain. He's referred to as the Father of New France, but he is both the founder of Québec and, I would also say, Canada. He has to be described as a true Canadian hero. However, he is not without controversy, which is exactly how we like our heroes in Canada—flawed!

He was born a Protestant, but in France he wasn't going anywhere unless he converted. And the man had some wanderlust. Nothing was going to stop him from, well, wandering. So, by the time he set off on his first voyage to Canada, he was Jewish. No, that's not right. He became Catholic. That's right! You needed to be Catholic to do anything in Catholic France. Champlain tagged along on several voyages to the New World and even became one of the founders of Port-Royal. Port-Royal was a small settlement in Acadia occupied only by men who kept each other's spirits up through the harsh winter by dressing like women and cooking for each other. Yep, yep, it does sound a bit gay. Anyways…

Next thing you know, Champlain's cruising the coast down to Cape Cod, making maps and figuring out the best places for settlement. I guess he'd done some good cooking, or whatever, back there at Port-Royal and laid the groundwork for this giant leap forward in terms of his career. I certainly can't speculate on what that groundwork was, though my mind is racing. I think he was also the first person to suggest that the tip of Cape Cod might one day become a gay Mecca. His employers weren't interested in that at the time. What they were interested in were furs. They were French, right? And what Frenchman doesn't like to be wrapped up in a little fur?

The year 1608 was a giant of a year in terms of Canada, Québec and New France, although you really don't need memorize that date. I mean, that's the way we are in Canada. Yes, the date's monumental, but I wouldn't want you to go out of your way in trying to remember it, even if you are trying to fake being one of us. As I've said before, those of us who are real Canadians don't really know these dates, although we do know what happened and who did it—sort of. So, what happened? Well, Champlain founded Québec. He established the city (where the river narrows) and it's bloody cold in the winter, but more than that, he set into motion everything that would make Québec the centre of New France and thus lead to the establishment of the country that you want to fake calling your own—Canada.

But this is where we also get a bit more controversial about the Father of Our Country. In founding Québec, Champlain made a bunch of deals—treaties—with the local St. Lawrence First Nations people as well as with those a little farther afield, including the Huron, who controlled the Great Lakes. The deals meant that when Champlain's First Nations allies went to war against their enemies, the Iroquois, the French were obliged to join in. Champlain, as an obliging ally and natural adventurer with modern weapons, joined his allies on a number of campaigns into Iroquois territory. Guess who won? In fact, Champlain was more than a little enthusiastic about these warring diversions. His allies were really happy to have him as a friend. The Iroquois, however, were not too thrilled with him or any of the French. You can imagine the kind of resentment this caused. I don't think Champlain knew exactly what he was getting himself, his people and his allies into. The Iroquois were a feisty and warlike bunch that were not going to shy away just because their enemies had joined up with funny-looking new-comers who had booming sticks and wore shiny metal tunics. What Champlain did by antagonizing the Iroquois was set in motion almost 100 years of war between the French and the Iroquois that led to the destruction of most of his First Nations allies and impeded the growth of New France. It wasn't entirely Champie's fault. I mean, how was he to know the Dutch and the English would give the Iroquois guns? Guess he hadn't figured out the old adage: "the enemy of my enemy is my friend." But the British had.

Champlain also did something that is more than a bit controversial today, except maybe for Celine Dion and her family. He married a 12-year-old Protestant girl. Marrying a 12-year-old wasn't that uncommon in the 17th century, but a Catholic marrying a Protestant was just not done. Unless secretly you were still a Protestant, however, I have no proof of this. The marriage didn't really work out, Champlain's wife returned to France without him and he was left with a big dowry, but no spouse. Just goes to prove that those May-December 1610 romances never work out. So Champlain threw himself back into his work. That was no surprise to his wife, who said all Champie ever talked about was Québec, Québec, Québec, never about her needs or her dollies or anything fun.

Anyway, as the wars continued, both domestically and with the Iroquois, Champlain built up the prosperity of Québec by setting up a nifty trading post with a bar and imported strippers from Normandy. Not really, but perhaps a little more love and less war would have done his cause better. Québec did become a thriving post where natives and French adventurers known as *coureurs de bois* (runners of the woods) came to sell their various fur pelts (beaver was big then). Everything was going really well, until war broke out between France and England. The English captured Québec, and Champlain was sent packing back to France.

Eventually, Québec was returned to French hands, and Champlain returned, appointed governor by Cardinal Richelieu himself. The little colony had just started getting back on its feet when Champlain died on December 25, 1635. Now of course, Champlain, being bigger than life itself, left more controversy behind when he died. In his will he bequeathed everything to the Virgin Mary. Because the Virgin Mary was already dead, his will was declared null and void. His heirs, including his wife, eventually got their various cuts of the Champlain estate. Ever since then, people have been trying to figure out where the great man is buried. They think what's left of him is somewhere there in Québec. So far, no conclusive old bones have showed up. Champlain had always played his personal life rather close to his tin-can tunic, so perhaps this is the way he wanted it. Besides, a little mystery has never hurt the legacy of any larger-than-life man. Just ask Jimmy Hoffa.

Britain and France Kick "Eh" Up a Notch

First, the Portuguese screwed themselves out of Canada with that whole Columbus debacle, and then the French had it done to them. That's right, the French, thanks to Cartier and Champlain and some others, built the northern New World into a thriving business enterprise with the fur trade. They laid the groundwork for doing over the First Nations and even established forts and contacts throughout the eastern half of the continent. Then came the British.

The British, who had been a rather sketchy and third-rate power in the European context of things, waited the others out and eventually became the dominant power in North America. They let the French clear much of the east for colonization and plunder purposes and then slowly moved in once they saw the continent was more than a little bankable. The British became allies with the Iroquois and supplied them with guns, resulting in the thinning of the proverbial First Nations herd, as it were. Which also meant fewer allies for the French. At the same time, they set up the Hudson's Bay Company and began to compete directly with the French in the fur trade. The British may have been slow to take to the continent, but once they did, their ambitions had no bounds.

Eventually, the grudge match between the Hudson's Bay Company and the French became annoying to the British. Once the timing was right, the British, along with the American colonies and the Iroquois, put the thumbscrews to the French. It all culminated in the 1759 Battle of the Plains of Abraham. You should remember this because it was a seminal event in terms of Canada's history. The Plains of Abraham is on the heights outside the walled city of Québec. The wily, though accident-prone, British General Wolfe had his forces scale the heights during the night. The next thing you knew, he and his men were engaged in armed combat with the French under the equally wily, though clumsy, General Montcalm. Twenty minutes later, Wolfe and Montcalm were dead, the British won the day and along with it, North America. The French as a colonial power were finished in Canada, although there was an attempted Gallic incursion with a speech by De Gaulle in the 1960s. But that's a subject for another day.

The French, however, were not finished as a people in Canada. The British, in their infinite wisdom, decided that instead of pushing the French colonists out and repopulating with some fine British stock, they would let the French colonists continue doing much of the tough work of settling the continent and basically giving the British pointers on how it was done. The British probably also had some inkling of the unrest that was mounting with the lower 13 colonies and thought perhaps Canada was a safe haven. The French colonials also had much straighter teeth than your average Brit, and the British still hadn't discovered dentistry.

For the most part, the French colonists remained. After all, though they spoke a similar language to those in France, the mother country hadn't done much for them lately—what with losing the continent and all. Mother France and her agents were also the original cause of the problem with the Iroquois, so perhaps the French colonists wanted to be on the winning side for once. So they said, "Mon Dieu! Let's see how it works out with the English pig-dogs!" They may also have chosen to stay because many of them were dirt poor—literally, all they owned was dirt—and they couldn't afford passage back to France. Besides, there was no regular transatlantic passenger traffic at the time, at least none that didn't often lead to the deaths of a third of the passengers. So, faced with the choice of hardship and death versus hardship and the British, they chose the British.

Not much else happened in Canada except further exploring, colonizing and the like until Québec received an almost, but not quite, tantalizing offer from the 13 Colonies:

> *Hey Québec, we've reserved you a spot in our really just rebellion against the imperial powers back in London. So, ah, whaddaya say? Wanna join us in a little whoop-ass against the Brits?*

Québec mulled the offer for as long as they could until finally the Americans demanded an answer.

> *Dear American Colonies:*
>
> *Thank you very much for your kind offer to join you in spilling more of our precious blood in a war against the British. However, you are slightly late. London has already guaranteed that we will be allowed to practice our language, customs and religion while remaining a British colony. There seems to be no reason, including, but not limited to, Hell freezing over, that would compel us to join you in your endeavour and thus take a chance on losing our culture and language rights in your new and really nifty American federation. We think we will instead continue our trapping and trading up here in the Great White North where we don't care if there are taxes on the tea—that oregano-like weed that we don't much care for.*
>
> *Thank you, bonne chance and up yours!*
>
> *Québec*

So in 1775, the Americans said, "Screw you, Québec!" and attacked. As you can see, the correspondence had deteriorated quite badly by then. However, some really thick walls, bad weather and obstinate French Canadians repulsed the attack, which turned into a major debacle for you, and when I say you, I mean your American ancestors.

The Québecois really didn't see the next thing coming: Americans, in the form of those still loyal to the British, started flooding into the northern colony. Next thing you knew, the French were a minority in the colony they had founded. Merde, merde, merde!

And Then the Fur Really Starts to Fly, Eh!

With the demise of French merchant-class influence in Canada, the Hudson's Bay Company thought it was going to be clear sailing when it came to its fur-trading business. But no. No sooner had the French been booted than their trade was taken over by a bunch of upstart Scottish merchants based in Montréal who called themselves the North West Company. The Nor'Westers and the HBC'ers settled into a long and often bitter struggle to control the fur trade. Luckily, it wasn't often bloody. The two companies and their employees often sniped at one another, copied one another or pulled pranks like fur-lined panty raids. And, believe me, if you've ever been involved in a fur-lined panty raid, you know the kind of acrimony that can cause, never mind the chafing.

Anyway, the result of the two chafed and bitter rivals being, well, rivals, was that Canada saw a whole lot of exploration. Always looking to one-up the other and set up a fort or get newly discovered First Nations people on their side, the companies' adventurous employees pushed ever farther west. The Nor'Westers were particularly good explorers—they didn't mind getting lost and asking directions, if the truth be told. The Hudson's Bay Co., as a longer established company, encouraged its employees to never ask, just take...or something like that, anyways. In fact, when hunters saw HBC's initials, they often interpreted them as "Here Before Christ." Now that's got to give you an overly inflated sense of yourself as a company, now doesn't it? People like Alexander Mackenzie and Simon Fraser,

working as Nor'Westers, finally pushed their way through the Rocky Mountains and found an overland route to the Pacific Ocean. The initial land routes were "pretty crappy," claimed the HBC people, and they were right, but the Nor'Westers had found them nonetheless.

Everything had settled into a nice little rivalry where everyone was getting rich—when I write everyone, I mean the guys at the top. The poor slobs at the bottom, slugging it out and doing the day-to-day hard work of trapping and trading, made a pittance, which of course is how poor slobs at the bottom have been paid throughout history. It was all pretty much like factory work by this point, except in the great outdoors and across vast spaces, where "punching in" usually had more to do with someone's face than a time clock. But in 1812, everything changed when the HBC set up the Red River Colony. The Red Riv…

…We Interrupt the Fur-Flying with a Misnamed War, Eh!

That's right, in the midst of the fun-loving rivalry of the fur set, war broke out! The war I'm referring to is, of course, the War of 1812, which should more accurately be called the War of 1812–14. With this one, Merry Olde England dropped us in the proverbial soup, or should I say toilet! I'm sure you can imagine what a Merry Olde English toilet of 1812 vintage was like. Awful! Well, it wasn't the first time Britain had leapt, and we paid the consequences. Nor would it be the last, but it just might be one of the most defining moments in Canadian history.

England was wrapped up in her own troubles at the time with the Napoleonic Wars back in Europe. Either because she couldn't see the forest for the trees, had her head in the kangaroo's pouch or just because she was one of the world's superpowers, Britain didn't much see or care how her actions were going to affect others. It's funny how superpowers then and now have this amazingly arrogant attitude about being the only people in the world who count: "So come on, help us!" says Britain. "Spill your blood for us, because it's really about helping you in the end…no, really! Hey, would we lie to you? Hey, it's us, Britain!"

As a result, the British Navy was being pretty indiscriminate about boarding neutral ships in their blockade of France, as well as naming names when it came to telling who the salty sea dogs had slept with. While boarding neutrals, the Limeys would sometimes find deserters from their own navy—deserters from the British Navy? I think not. Oh, no, it's true!—and then press them back into service. Determining who was British and who wasn't was pretty difficult back then, since sailors rarely carried passports, birth certificates or even knew whom their fathers were. As a result, some Americans were wrongly pressed into British naval service. Well, as you can imagine, your American ancestors, only 30 years on from winning their independence, were pretty incensed that their former overseers were having their proverbial captain's way with the wee lass of an American nation and her seagoing citizens.

So, war was declared. Well, not only because of the various exchanges of seamen. Although Americans don't often like to admit this, sometimes there are unscrupulous peoples in your midst or Congress who have ulterior motives, sometimes involving making an extra, illegal, or at all costs buck. So this was the case when a group known as the War Hawks swept the Congress up in a frenzy over all the seamen incidents.

The War Hawks could have cared less about the seamen, their families or rubber thingys on their sailors' dingys. What the War Hawks really wanted was to drive the British from North America because they saw it as America's "Manifest Destiny" to rule the continent and their God-given right to plunder its riches for their own personal and business profit. They also thought it was "just a real boss time" to stick it to the British while they were already engaged in a war back on the Continent.

So War it Was.

Oddly enough, the War Hawks and their buds didn't have much of a plan for the war except for the moment when the president could land on an aircraft carrier and stand beneath a sign declaring "Mission Accomplished!" The resulting conflict saw a war of two steps forward and three steps back over and over again in what can only be described as cha-cha manoeuvrings. What you should take from this, as Aspiring Reasonable Facsimiles of Canadians, is that again and again and again, American forces were repulsed. I'm talking bruised, bloodied and soiling in their pants, beaten badly to a pulp and worse.

A British general named Sir Isaac Brock beat the American forces back so badly at Queenston Heights that he is referred to as the "Saviour of Upper Canada." Upper Canada was the name given to what is the present-day province of Ontario. But in Lower Canada (present-day Québec), things were no different. British troops, along with French Canadian militias and First Nations allies, wiped the floor with America's fledgling army. In the middle of all this, York (present-day Toronto) was burned twice by American forces, and the president's residence in Washington was torched by the British in a sort of White House bonfire of your American vanities.

The result of the war was a draw, which can really only mean a victory for Britain and an even greater victory for Canada. For with this war, all the disparate interests of the British North

American colonies came together to stave off an American onslaught and, as a result, forge the beginnings of our nation. We would always have the attitude, more or less, "In your face, America! We beat you, we're superior and we're not just up north!" But we would display this only in a quiet, unassuming and very neighbourly way.

As a side note, although you needn't remember it, one of the young, Congressional War Hawks who pushed for the war was a man named Dick Cheney. Not quite 200 years later, he would still be on the scene pushing another war as vice president. Okay, it's not true, but it is something that wouldn't be too hard to believe, eh?

...Now Back to the Fur Wars, Eh!

Just as the War of 1812–14 was getting started, the war between the Hudson's Bay Company and the North West Company was also heating up. That's right, two wars, no waiting. Actually, the fur conflict didn't heat up to the level of war until after the 1812–14 war ended, and I have to say it was very nice of the furries to wait their turn.

Basically, the HBC tried to set up a colony along the Red River that covered areas in what are now Manitoba, North Dakota and Minnesota. They called it Assiniboia, because "boya, were they going to be doin' a sinnin' way out there." Not really, but I'm sure they did do some sinning. So, the Nor'Westers and their Métis buds didn't take to the newcomers who were so blatantly trying to horn in on their profitable area of the fur trade. They kept trying to thwart the efforts of the new settlers and the Hudson's Bay Company in general.

The Hudson's Bay Company settlers and their governor Robert Semple didn't much care for the Métis and confronted them at Seven Oaks in 1816. The result? Semple and 20 other Red River colonists died. The colonists weren't that skilled at open warfare on the plains, and the Métis were—they lost only one man.

After that, there were more skirmishes, and the HBC even seized the North West Company's post at Fort William (modern-day Thunder Bay, Ontario). However, it all came crashing down, or more accurately went out with a whimper, when the Hudson's Bay Company and the North West Company merged. The war was over, bitter enemies were now friends and money was made by all. Although that would not be the last time the Red River Colony saw an uprising.

If They Can Have an Uprising, Eh, We'll Have a Rebellion

And that's the way it went back in the Canadas. They were not going to be outdone by some penny ante outpost on the Red River, no sirree, Bob…What's that? How did I know your name is Bob? I'm psychic that way.

As I was saying, unrest was fomenting in the Canadas. By 1791, the colony of Québec had been divided into two colonies: Upper Canada and Lower Canada. Upper Canada consisted of the area now known as Southern Ontario. Lower Canada was that part of modern-day Québec surrounding the St. Lawrence River and stretching north and east to include most of present-day Labrador and everything south to the Atlantic colonies and America's northern border. The two Canadas were apparently given the names "Lower" and "Upper" because Lower Canada lay along the lower section of the St. Lawrence River, and Upper Canada lay along the uppermost part of the river and beyond. However, if you look on a map, Lower Canada is clearly positioned higher up than Upper Canada. This little oddity is a puzzle to most school-age Canadian children because for them, like most of us, the names would make more sense if they were switched. Upper Canada is clearly located farther south, so it should be called Lower Canada, *n'est-ce pas*? However, I believe—and I think a great many people would agree with me—that Lower Canada, being mostly populated by Catholic French-speaking people, was given the inferior or "Lower" title

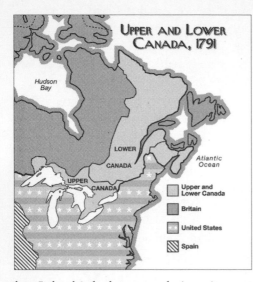

to keep its people firmly in their place and under thumb. The Protestant and mostly English-speaking Upper Canada was awarded the prestigious "Upper" designation to imply, if not out-and-out say, that Upper Canadians were the superior lot. It may seem childish and silly, but I do think the name designations smack of racism that could only have been perpetrated by the less-than-subtle and clearly uncreative British.

The great thing about this racist division of the Canadas is that it didn't last long. There was unrest in both colonies, and reformers in both places got pretty cozy with one another. In your face, Mother England!

By 1837, the common people in both Canadian colonies were ready for change. They wanted a real say over their lives and governance, but the British, in the form of the colonial governors, refused. The lesson the Brits had taken from their trouncing in the American Revolution was that the common people shouldn't be given power. Odd? Makes you think the Brits of the time were a bit slow, overly inbred or just plain arrogant. So rebellion broke out all over the Canadas like pimples on a teenage boy's face. Actually, it wasn't quite that bad, but rebellion it was… well for the most part. Some of it was impolite grumbling. But grumbling can be annoying…if not rebellious.

Things got a lot more heated in Lower Canada than in Upper Canada. In Lower Canada, there were no less than three armed uprisings around Montréal. Twenty-seven soldiers and 300 reformers, known as Patriotes, died. In Upper Canada, the insurrection was, more or less, a bunch of drunkards stumbling out of Montgomery's Tavern and winding their way down Yonge Street toward Toronto. The drunkard reformers were armed mostly with pitchforks and clubs, though a few had guns. Some shots were fired by both the reformers and the local militia but no one was about to die for the cause. The reformers basically ran away. Now, I know what you Americans are thinking: how do you call something a rebellion when the rebels run away screaming "Oh, mommy, mommy, save me!"? Well, you link it to the same time period as the real armed insurrection in Lower Canada and then ride on that feisty little rebellion's coattails.

The result of the Rebellions of 1837, as they are known, was that the rebel leaders in both Canadas, Louis Joseph Papineau and William Lyon Mackenzie (who I like to call William "Running Away Like a Little Girl" Mackenzie), fled to the United States. Some Patriotes in Lower Canada and Reformers in Upper Canada were arrested and sent packing to Australia, and a few others were even executed. More people were executed in Lower Canada because firearms were actually involved. Fewer rebels were executed in Upper Canada because hanging someone whose back is the only thing you can identify is difficult and seems like it might be bad luck.

That wasn't the end, though. The British sent in Lord Durham to figure out what the heck the problem was, and he came back with a nifty little report. I think it might have even been tied up with big bows and decorated with neatly curlicued fringes. Lord Durham's highly opinionated, although less than thoroughly researched, report said the French in Lower Canada were a backward people. I guess you're backward in a British

Lord's eyes if you don't see the sense of letting the few rule over the many. I mean, just look at the debacle the French Revolution turned out to be! So to curb French influence, he proposed that the two Canadas should be united into one colony so that the French would be outnumbered, outvoted and lose all influence. Lord Durham was clearly an idiot, although the other recommendation he made was not so far off. He suggested the new colony should have something called "responsible government." That's a system in which an elected assembly controls the government. Pretty wacky thing for a lord to come up with, and the Brits didn't much like it. They went with Lord Durham's first recommendation and passed on the second, clearly showing that the Brits in general, and their envoy Lord Durham in particular, were all one in the same in terms of idiocy.

So by 1841, the two Canadas became the united province of Canada, and within a decade, that wacky concept of "responsible government" had been achieved.

And Then Came Sir John Eh, and His Fathers of Confederation Travelling Show... Laser Lights Extra

Olde Mother England became a lot less interested in us after "responsible government" took hold and we started making our own decisions. Or it might just have been that she was way too wrapped up in the two or three undergarments one had to wear during the Victorian Age. It was quite repressive. Oh, and that Queen Victoria, what an old, ugly bag she turned out to be! Whatever the reasons, disinterest or old bag fatigue, Britain started pushing her various North American colonies together like a well-seasoned matchmaker.

"Hey, United Provinces of Canada, wouldn't you like to date New Brunswick?"

"Well, she is kind of cute, but we like how Nova Scotia's itty-bitty head comes off in the form of Cape Breton Island. That's hot!"

Unlike the nasty, disruptive and terribly violent struggle the U.S. had to fight against Britain for its freedom, Britain just kept encouraging Canada to leave. Perhaps the lesson is if you wait long enough, a violent struggle or war isn't necessary. It could also be that if you're the ugly duckling of the bunch, always complaining, never listening and kind of frigid, the mother bird eventually gets tired of your squawking and pushes you out of the nest. Then she pretends it was an accident while she lets you fall next to a large, powerful and sometimes dim-witted elephant that often doesn't see you and that the mother bird hopes will crush you. Well, the elephant hasn't crushed us yet, though there have been some close calls. So, in your face, ugly-old-crone–producing Victorian England!

The United Province of Canada could take a hint. Besides, the French and English elements in Canada East and Canada West had learned to work together for reform and soon started looking for partnerships outside the province.

Canada came into being on July 1, 1867, thanks to some nifty political manoeuvring by a Scottish-born Canadian lawyer and politician named John A. Macdonald. He isn't the only Father of Confederation, as our founding fathers are called, but he was the man! It only took three meetings over about three years to put together the new country. Sir John A. put together a low-cost package deal—he was in the package-deal business—that included trips to Charlottetown, PEI; Québec City, Québec; and London, England. Many people put Sir John A's success down to the fact he was a great listener and organizer, but I personally think it had more to do with his fondness for whiskey. The man loved to drink, and you have to know he bent more than a few elbows buying rounds for everyone to get his "let's make a new country" deal to fly.

In the end, or more accurately, in the beginning, New Brunswick, Nova Scotia and Canada merged to become the Dominion of Canada. Sir John A. wanted to call it the Kingdom of Canada, but Victoria and her upper echelon advisors thought that name might anger the Americans. And God forbid we should ever anger those sensitive Americans.

Anyway, the new country or dominion as it was called because it wasn't entirely a country yet, consisted of four provinces: Nova Scotia, New Brunswick, Québec and Ontario. Canada wasn't officially a stand-alone country since our former motherland still held the apron strings on a number of key issues. As became clear during the Alaska Boundary Dispute, (or the Big British Columbia Hosing as we call it here—see the BC section for details), we couldn't negotiate treaties on our own. Our constitution also remained in Britain, and we had to go there and get British approval to make changes to it. And let's face it, it costs a lot of money for a big almost-country like Canada to traipse off back to Europe so Mom can say yes, no or maybe to our requests.

We took little steps closer and closer to complete autonomy during the next 115 years until Prime Minister Trudeau finally repatriated our Constitution in 1982. So, in practice and in theory, we are finally a whole—or is that a hole?—country, free to do anything as we please. Of course, we live next to the United States, so we have to be careful what we do or say because it is so sensitive about the least little thing: "No, we're not going to help you attack Iraq, but you're still our bestest buddy, right?" Then again, is any country completely free to do whatever it wants whenever it wants? Sorry, except for the United States, that is.

And Now a Note on Government and Politics in Canada. Don't Groan, Eh! I Know It's Boring, but I'll Make It Short. You Have to Know Something About It if You Want to Pretend to Be One of Us.

The Fathers of Confederation (FOCs) were in a hurry to get this whole Canadian experiment going, so instead of formulating a new type of government, they coasted, went with what they knew and chose the British model. Does anyone want to hazard a guess as to why they didn't go with the French model? Nope, it was not an anti-France bias. That came later after we, along with you Americans, saved their French butts in World War II and they repaid us by having De Gaulle come here in the 1960s and stick his big nose in where it didn't belong! Ahem…

Well, of course, the reason the FOCs didn't go with the French model of government was actually because they looked at government types on a Sunday and chose one on a Monday. It was a long weekend, so the French were on an EU-endorsed holiday and couldn't possibly make a presentation until 1945. So the FOCs never found out exactly what the details were behind the French model of government.

The British model is a constitutional monarchy, or farce for short. Actually it's not officially referred to as a farce, but it is often laughable. With a constitutional monarchy, you are obliged to have a monarch as your head of state. Some of the newer dudes in government wanted the head of state to be a monarch butterfly, but that idea never got off the ground. Instead, we just adopted the British monarch, which means that currently Queen Elizabeth II is our head of state. Now, she doesn't get involved in the day-to-day stuff of being the head of state of Canada. Instead, she has a representative here in Canada, called the Governor General, who does all the grunt work day in and day out: waving, having teas and signing his or her name. He or she lives at the official residence of the Governor General in Ottawa, which is called Rideau Hall. The Governor General can be a man or a woman, though apparently not both. The Queen only fulfills her gig as Canada's head of state when she is actually in Canada. That is almost never. Let's face it, she's already got a lot to do in Britain with being the head of state there and managing those ugly, brain-dead children she bore by that craggy-faced Philip. I mean, His Royal Highness, the Duke of Edinburgh.

Canada is also a federal state, not unlike the U.S. Down south, there is a federal government, and then each state has its own government. Up here it's quite similar, with a federal government and each province having its own government. Our federal government is similar to the American version in that it is also quite big and ineffective. I should also point out that our federal government is similar to the two Houses of Congress in the U.S. We too have two houses, the Dog House and the Dung Heap. Not really. They're called the House of Commons and the Senate, and together with the monarch they make up our parliamentary democracy. Of the two houses of parliament, only the House of Commons is a democratically elected body. At least every five years, an election has to be called, mud-slinging begins and we all have to trudge off to the local school gymnasium to mark an X for a candidate who we hope doesn't rob us blind. It's similar to your congressional elections, I guess.

The political party that receives the most seats in the election takes up those seats on the government side of the House of Commons, and their leader becomes Prime Minister—the head of government. We have had some real potato heads in that position over the years. The prime minister gets all the perks and an official residence thrown in. It's called 24 Sussex Drive, which is actually its address in Ottawa. The prime minister chooses a cabinet from his or her ablest members of parliament (MPs) or closest buddies, and they set about running, ruining or bitch-slapping the country. Members of other parties take up their seats opposite the government in the House of Commons and are called the opposition. The leader of the opposition is the head of the party with the second highest number of seats in the House of Commons—the Official Opposition. The leader of the opposition also gets an official (paid for by tax-payers) residence. It is called Stornoway. It's not quite as nice as 24 Sussex, but hey, it's free.

The second house of parliament is the Senate. The Senate is often referred to as the "house of sober second thought," which is funny because senators are most often drunk. Well, I can't prove that, but they could be, since senators are not elected but instead are appointed by the prime minister and serve until age 75 or death, whichever comes first. However, there have been a few occasions where dead senators were still serving but nobody noticed. That's because the Senate is the place where the old warhorses of Canadian politics get a cushy job in their twilight years. They get to sleep a lot in a big red room, reminisce about their glory days and even hang out naked together in a Finnish-style sauna…ewww! Seats in the Senate/sauna chamber are wooden so that the old guys' naked skin doesn't stick to them. Okay the Senate chamber isn't a sauna; it's actually more of a daycare for the geriatric set.

Seats in the Senate are apportioned on a regional basis. In theory, the Senate is supposed to look at all government legislation, talk about it and vote on it with the emphasis on how it affects each region, the idea being that then no specific region will get screwed or get all the perks. In practice, the Senate is just a rubber stamp for the government. They sometimes make suggestions on laws, but the few times they have actually tried to overrule the governing party in the House of Commons, there has been hell to pay. So, most of the time, the old guys and gals of the Senate just hang around, say yea and rarely nay, and have conversations like:

"Oh Roland, I think I'm about to die of boredom."

"Too late, Frank. You died last week."

"Oh…Is our free lunch coming yet?"

Canadian Political Parties and How Not to Get Drunk With Power and Piss-off The People, Eh!

There are three major national political parties in Canada. They are as follows:

- The Liberal Party: The party is traditionally identified by the colour red. Members are sometimes referred to as Grits, as in kiss my…. They have been the ruling party in federal politics more often than not. Pierre Elliot Trudeau, our prime minister during the 1970s, was a Liberal, as was our longest serving prime minister, William Lyon Mackenzie King. King was a former academic and remained a bachelor his entire life. He was inordinately close to both his mother and his dog. After they died, he tried to contact each of them during séances. Our 1990s Prime Minister, Jean Chrétien, was also a Liberal. He wasn't inordinately close to his mother or his dog, but he does have the dubious honour of speaking both our official languages extremely badly. Is this an equal opportunity country or what?

- The Conservative Party: The party is traditionally identified by the colour blue. Party members are often referred to as Tories. Yes, that's right, the same evil Tories that you Americans ousted from your country during your revolution. The Tories all moved up here under the guise of United Empire Loyalists and took up the mantle of the Conservative Party. The party has been through a number of name changes over the years. This is mainly due to upstart political parties who took votes away from the Tories. The Tories would wait for a time and then merge with the new party with a hyphenated name. All in all

PAUL MARTIN, JACK LAYTON AND STEPHEN HARPER

though, the party would remain the same old Tory party—staunch conservatives, you know the kind. They merged with the Progressive Party in the 1940s and were known as the Progressive Conservative Party (PCs) into the 1990s. That's when old Big Bri from Baie Comeau, that is, Brian Mulroney, so alienated the people of Canada that his party suffered its biggest trouncing in history. They were turfed from office. Then the Reform Party, a righter-than-right Western rights party, began taking votes away from the PCs. Eventually, the Reform Party became the Canadian Alliance Party, and the Canadian Alliance Party merged with the PCs. Then the party returned to its earlier name of the Conservative Party. The Conservatives have been known to fight almost as much among themselves as attack those from other parties. They usually do themselves in, which is, of course, what we are currently waiting for. Conservatives of note? Our first prime minister, Sir John A. Macdonald, was a Conservative. The party must have been a lot different back then—and lubricated liberally with whiskey—because it was the Liberal-Conservative party at the time. With all the name changes, one has to wonder what that party is hiding...

- The New Democratic Party (NDP): The party is traditionally identified by the colour yellow, or sort of an off-yellow that looks a bit like the cheese you find in Kraft Dinner (see the Food section for an explanation of Kraft Dinner). Officially, the party says its colours are orange and green—kind of a light lime green, actually. The New Democratic Party has the strongest left-leaning social democratic philosophy of all the major parties, though most of Canada's parties have a social democratic aspect to them. So, how new is the New Democratic Party? It was founded in 1961, so it's more than 40 years old, which I'd say is pretty old for a party that calls itself new. Perhaps it's time for a new name? However, the NDP was previously called the Cooperative Commonwealth Federation (CCF). Sounds a bit commie, doesn't it? Especially to you Americans, huh? The CCF was founded in the 1930s and saw some success in provincial politics, especially in Saskatchewan. The former provincial premier of Saskatchewan, Tommy Douglas, became the first leader of the NDP in 1961. By the way, Tommy Douglas was the grandfather of actor Kiefer Sutherland, who plays Jack Bauer on the American TV show *24*. Tommy Douglas was also recently voted "The Greatest Canadian" on a CBC television show called, surprise, *The Greatest Canadian*. The NDP has never won the most seats in a federal election, so there has never been a prime minister from the party. However, the NDP has played a major role in keeping various Liberal governments afloat and was

responsible for introducing socialised medicine to Canada.
We are pretty much all grateful for that!

- There is one other major party in the federal arena,
although it is not a national party. It is, however, a national
pain in the ass! It's called the Bloc Québecois, and it is
a left-of-centre political party represented by a light blue
colour. The Bloc, as it is referred to, only runs candi-
dates in Québec and is dedicated to obtaining sovereignty
for that province…as long as they still get their Canadian-
government pensions, that is. Okay, I've brought it down to
a basic, although true, level. So spank me! I know you want
to, Blocquistes! The Bloc was started in 1990 and has
pretty much been winning the majority of federal seats in
Québec ever since. In terms of ordinary people in the rest
of Canada, in some ways the Bloc has been a pretty good
thing since it, like the NDP, has a socialist agenda. Up with
people, woohoo! In 1993, the Bloc won the second largest
number of seats in the House of Commons and became the
Official Opposition. That was interesting and embarrassing
for the other opposition parties, but it didn't last.

There are also several other political parties on the national
scene, but none have ever won votes in a major way, so you
needn't worry about them.

And Now Back to Our Regularly Scheduled History Lesson, or a Funny Thing Happened after We Became a Country, Eh?

Actually, it's not funny at all. It's mostly dull. For some reason,
after a place becomes a country (or Dominion/pseudo-country),
it becomes a lot less interesting. I guess countries are like people
that way. Because when people become countries, well you
hardly recognize them. They get complacent, stop working out
and they eat way too much. Before you know it, they balloon up
to the size of Marlon Brando after *The Godfather*. They also start

to talk without opening their mouths, then they kiss Larry King on the lips and man-oh-man, they're just dull, dull, dull! Next thing you know, their credo is all about "peace, order and good government" and what can I say about that except what an über-dull, yet relatively stable place Canada became with that credo.

You, as Aspiring Reasonable Facsimiles of Canadians, should remember the phrase "peace, order and good government" not only because it's dull, but also because it is our equivalent of the American "truth, honour and the American way." No, that's not right, I think that's Superman's motto. Okay, okay, I've got it now. Our "peace, order and good government," POGG for short, is equal to the U.S. "life, liberty and the pursuit of happiness." LLATPOH? Hmmm…it's always been beyond me why Americans had to enshrine the ideas of life and pursuing happiness in an official declarative document. To us in Canada, these things go without saying. Although, I will have to admit, times were a bit different 100 years earlier when they were form-ing the U.S. than they were in 1867 when we kind of put some of the pieces of our jigsaw puzzle together. However, perhaps if they'd enshrined the idea of good government in the Declaration of Independence, Americans might have gotten a good one. What am I saying? We've enshrined it, or more accurately Britain enshrined it for us, and we're still waiting for the good govern-ment to appear. As I've written a few times before, Canadians are nothing if not patient!

Anyway, the point of all of this is that the rest of your history lesson is going to be quick because although many things hap-pened over the 140 years since we became (kind of) a country, most of it is dull! Or alternatively, most of our 140-year history is only interesting to a few people, and most of those people also believe in UFOs and Bigfoot.

Hey Canada, Have I Got a Deal for You, Eh!

So, Canada was up and running in a country-like manner. It had four provinces, a whole lot of natural resources and the optimism of all countries that are just starting out on their own. Sure, it had been rejected by Prince Edward Island, but Canadians were not going to let that put a damper on things. Besides, they had a feeling Prince Edward Island would come crawling back to them, cap in hand, saying: "Ya know what boys? I think we were a little bit hasty in 1867. Whaddaya say we joins ya in y'ur newfangled country now, eh?" But that would have to wait until 1873.

Even as Canadians celebrated pseudo-nationhood on July 1, 1867, the movers and shakers in the government were looking at expansion. So, they decided, "Hey, that United States looks pretty well founded, and if we sweep in there all quiet-like at night with our massive army, I think we can take it over before sunrise." The glitch in the plan was, of course, the fact that Canada didn't have a massive army. Otherwise, I think we can safely say that the United States of America experiment would have ended, and Canada would have had a fifth province called Downthereland, or something.

So instead, the government of the day looked to pastures they could take over relatively easily. When they looked west, they saw a whole lot of untamed land, a few Natives and some Métis and decided, "Bing, bang, boom, there it is for sure, yessirree Bob!" In what has been dubbed the "Bing, Bang, Boom, There It Is For Sure, Yessirre Bob! Declaration," Canada headed to the nearest Hudson's Bay trading post, and by the time it had made its way through the checkout line, it owned the North-West Territories and a nifty HBC blanket to boot. Not exactly how it happened, but pretty close. For £300,000 and a little bit of land, Canada more than doubled its size. The area of land purchased included all of what today includes Yukon, Alberta, Saskatchewan, Manitoba, the northern parts of Ontario and Québec and most of the Northwest Territories and Nunavut. The vast area was called the North-West Territories, except for a small square in the southeast, which was called Manitoba. And that's when another rebellion broke out.

The Red River Rebellion and Louis Riel, Part *Un* (One), Eh!

In their rush to buy up the Hudson's Bay Company's land in the west and create a new province around the Red River settlement, the fledgling Canadian government forgot to consider that their actions might affect people's lives. They were being all British or American about it—no offence intended. You know, "Hey man, we bought the land fair and square, so we'll do with it what we want!" The Red River settlers (who had been nothing but problems for the Hudson's Bay Company from the beginning) were continuing their tradition of being, let's say, outwardly hostile. The people most concerned about the new province were the Métis, who if you remember from their fighting at Seven Oaks, were not shy about asserting their rights. They and their leader, Louis Riel, thought they were going to get hosed during the creation of the new province and would probably lose their land and rights. So, instead of sitting back and waiting to see how honourably the Canadian government would deal with them, they locked down the colony and set up their own provisional government.

Everything was going along just fine, and Riel was even negotiating with the Canadian government, when a troublemaking loudmouth named Thomas Scott led an attempt to overthrow of the provisional government. It failed because, although Scott was a loudmouth, he wasn't much of planner. He and his people were imprisoned, but he wouldn't shut up and eat his three squares of pemmican a day. Soon Scott faced court martial by the provisional government, but he refused to be intimidated and continued to bellyache, carry on and be a really belligerent pain. So the provisional government executed him. Oops!

There was outrage in Ontario, so the federal government sent in the military. Riel and many others fled Red River, and on July 1, 1870, Manitoba became a province. However, that would not be the last time Louis Riel made Canadian history interesting.

The Mounties Get the Nod, Eh!

A territory the size of the North-West Territories required men of iron to combat lawlessness. So the federal government employed a high-end fashion designer, and abracadabra, red tunics were knitted and the North-West Mounted Police were born. Their first big task was to get to the North-West Territories. Heading to Fort Whoop-Up and beyond, the Mounties' "Great March West," as it is called, was less than great, although mostly westerly in direction. The Mounties endured a 1300-kilometre saunter across the Prairies during a major heat wave. The not-so-starry trek took three months, horses died and in the end, they had to stop and get directions—and you know how men hate to ask directions. Okay, it wasn't the most auspicious beginning, but it was definitely Canadian. The North-West Mounted Police also eventually morphed into the RCMP. That so-called morphing is perhaps a case of trying to cover past embarrassing tracks.

Then Came Batoche—Louis Riel, Part *Deux* (Two), Eh!

Because of the messiness of the Red River Rebellion, Louis Riel was officially banished from Canada for five years. (Oh, banished? Well, that is a terrible punishment!) He ended up living in Montana. (Okay, that's a bit different. Now I feel sorry for him.) During his five years in exile and a subsequent nine years, Riel led a really busy life: he suffered a nervous breakdown, got delusions of grandeur, thought he was a prophet of God sent to Earth to set up the Bishop of Montréal as the Pope of the New World, ran for Parliament and won, moved to the United States, got married, joined the Republican party, became an American citizen and started teaching school at a mission in Montana. So what if he'd once been the head of the provisional government back at Red River? The man was not going to rest on those laurels forever.

In 1884, when a group of Métis sought Riel's help to press their land claims in the Saskatchewan Valley, he loaded up the family and moved back to Canada. Then he started his agitatin' ways again. He used petitions and letters to press the land-claims case and was again seeing some success, until his patience ran out and he returned to his old, yet comfortable conclusion that he was the Prophet of the New World. He and some of his Métis followers clashed with a much smaller force of North-West Mounted Police at Duck Lake. That's right, the nut took on the Mounties—and won. The North-West Rebellion was on!

In a move repeated from his old days back in Red River, Riel set up a provisional government. This time, though, the federal government was in no mood to negotiate. It sent 8000 troops by train on some freshly laid tracks. The army defeated Riel's Métis lickety-split, and the North-West Rebellion was over almost before it started. The only thing left was the trial and subsequent hanging of Riel, which took place scarcely six months later. The lasting effects of Riel and his two rebellions have had a ripple effect down through Canada's history. That is, of course, how the ripple chip was invented, though people scarcely talk about it, and it isn't at all true. Actually the ripple effect was a lasting distrust between English and French. In Québec, Riel was seen as a hero who fought for the rights of a French minority. In Ontario, Riel was seen as a dangerous traitor. As for the Métis and other indigenous peoples, they pretty much learned not to trust any of us and tried to move farther west.

The Great War and Canada's Seat at the Kiddie Table

We, like many nations, were full participants in World War I— meaning we got slaughtered in the trenches along with the rest. Unlike some nations who came to the fight rather late and then claimed they won the whole thing, we were there from the beginning. But please don't applaud. We had no choice. Britain declared war, and we were automatically in it. Remember how I said we weren't a full country yet? Here's another example of that.

Now there's not much doubt that we would have entered the fight, but Britain said, "Hey Canada, war's on and you're fighting for us. So send us some of your young men since we need cannon fodder, oh, and be quick about it. How many can we put you down for?" That didn't sit well with a great many people, although we did actually send those young men. The commanders in the field were going through men like they were sugar cubes at a high tea, and the Canadian government was forced to introduce the draft, or conscription as we call it in Canada. That's where a real problem began, because conscription really didn't sit well with everyone in Canada—especially people in Québec.

The same year that conscription was introduced (1917), Canadians won a triumph when we finally fought a battle as a separate and distinct unit. Before that, we were always under the command of the British. This time, Canadian commanders planned the attack and Canadian soldiers—with some support from the British—successfully executed it. That was at Vimy Ridge, where there is now a rather large war memorial to Canada's soldiers.

The result of Canadian successes (or losses depending on your perspective) was that we were given a seat at the table when it came time to negotiate the Versailles Treaty. It's too bad that for our first time at the table, the results turned out so poorly, but we can hardly be blamed for that. Yes, we had a seat at the table, but we certainly weren't on the dais. In fact, the table we were at was more like the kiddy table, which Canada had been promoted to, Portugal had been relegated to and Japan dutifully sat at (but they would get back at the world for that humiliation in the next war).

Canada Really Gets a Say and the War in Europe—The Sequel

Things were a lot different for Canada in World War II than had been the case in 1914. Well, it wasn't actually that different except in terms of when and how we entered the conflict. In 1914, we were automatically dragged into it because Britain said so. Not so in 1939. Britain declared war on Germany on September 3, 1939, but we let them sweat it out for a time on their own. Okay, they had the French with them, but as it turned out, they may as well have been on their own. I don't mean to offend the French, but they folded faster than…I don't know…the French in World War II. I know that sounds redundant, but there really is no better metaphor. Britain was on its own in the fight against Germany for almost seven days until Canada ponied up on September 10. It was more a political gesture to show our own independence than a serious attempt at making Britain sweat. No, really. I mean if we'd really wanted to make Britain sweat we'd have waited maybe two years or so, until 1941, to join in. But we didn't. Unlike some.

Canada's contribution to the war effort is something that makes all Canadians proud. The only thing that puts a damper on it is our treatment of Japanese Canadians during the war years. They were fingerprinted and later removed from their homes on the West Coast and interred in camps. Many of them lost everything they owned before the war. We also didn't win any prizes for how we treated many Ukrainians, Mennonites and a whole host of others.

Some 700,000 Canadians served in the armed forces during World War II, and Canada became the centre for training pilots and aircrews for Commonwealth countries during the war. Canadians participated in campaigns in Sicily, Italy, Hong Kong and Normandy, and we liberated much of Holland.

Newfoundland Joins the Party

By 1949, Newfoundland had tired of playing coy in terms of joining Canada. With Premier Joey Smallwood (a giant of a man
who was not really wooden at all) leading the charge,
Newfoundland (including Labrador) finally joined in the
Canadian experiment. It was the last piece of the Canadian
puzzle to be added, but certainly not the least. And I didn't
write that because I'm sucking up or it's the law or anything.
I mean, it's true. Really. I can't say what part is the least,
because the law prohibits me from doing so, but it does start
with an N or a B or an A, P, S, M, Y or Q. Know what I mean?

A Flag, A Birthday and a Swingin' PM

The 1960s were a swingin' time, baby, and for Canada, swingin'
wasn't the half of it. I'm not sure what the half of it was, but
it wasn't swingin'. In 1965, we got a brand new flag that was
nothing if not unexciting. That's right, I mean it wasn't exciting.
Who gets excited about a flag, really? Most people don't care
whether you wave it, hang it upside down at a hockey game or
even boo it. (Most people, that is.) Our official Canadian flag,
as I'm sure you know as Aspiring Reasonable Facsimiles of
Canadians and our great neighbours, is red and white and has
a pointy red maple leaf in the centre. I'm not really sure what
else can be said about the flag, except perhaps, "Neato!"

The flag wasn't the end of our swingin '60s experience though.
In 1967, Canada celebrated 100 years as a nation. Of course it
was kind of a ruse because we weren't fully a nation during that
time, as I've explained previously. In fact, in 1967, if we wanted
to make changes to our constitution, we still had to head back
over to England and say. "Hey, British Parliament, we'd like to
make a change, please, please, please, please, please!" Officially,
the five "pleases" weren't necessary, but we'd learned long ago
that fake politeness greased the wheels with the British, especially if we looked up at them with the naïve eyes of a child.

We'd perfected the look by this time, but even to us, it was wearing a bit thin. (See the section on Canadian Politeness for more details.)

So Montréal was the site of our big 100th birthday party, although we still hadn't fully been birthed, or hatched, or set free or something. It gets a bit complicated, so don't worry too much about the details because most Canadians don't. The World's Fair, Expo '67, with the theme "Man and his World," was the highlight of our centennial celebrations. All the hip, happening and swingin' countries were there, and man did they spend some cash trying to outdo one another. America's pavilion was fun and had Buckminster Fuller's geodesic dome and the world's longest escalator. The Russians spent their little communist hearts out throwing together a spectacular pavilion that highlighted every USSR innovation they could lay claim to and then some. Were they trying just a little too hard? I can't say. In total, 50 million more-than-satisfied people attended Expo '67. We definitely spared no expense in throwing ourselves a big birthday bash. Of course, a scant nine years later, our birthday bash seemed quaint next to the unbelievably over-the-top and gaudy show (yes, I'm jealous) put on for the 200th birthday bash of the U.S. But then again, Canadians have never been ones to toot our own horns the way Americans do. At least not in public—we save that kind of thing for the bedroom.

Speaking of bedrooms, "The state has no place in the bedrooms of the nation," is how a young and charismatic minister of justice named Pierre Trudeau characterized his massive and dare I say, swingin' big-time overhaul of Canada's criminal code in 1967. The changes to the law decriminalized homosexuality and other sexual acts as long as they were behind closed doors. Public acts still had to be okayed by doctors and politicians first at conventions and swingers' parties, but what adults consented to do with each other behind closed doors had no bounds.

The following year, Mr. Trudeau rode that sexy law into the prime minister's seat, which does not in any way, shape or form imply that the prime minister's seat is sexy or taut or tight. Ahem.... That, of course, would involve an evaluation of every prime minister's seat. And except for Mr. Trudeau's seat, at least in those early years, who wants to look at a prime minister's seat? Ewww!

Canada's War on Terror

That's right, you know this "War On Terror" that your President Bush claims to be fighting? Well, he didn't invent the fight. Way back in 1970, Canada saw homegrown terrorists' faces that donned bushy beards and really weren't very attractive. But I'm sure that had nothing to do with what caused them to wear ski masks, skulk about and use violence in demanding independence for Québec. The terrorists, under the banner of the FLQ (Front de Liberation du Québec, or Québec Liberation Front), kidnapped the British trade commissioner, James Cross, in Montréal in October 1970. Within a week, the group also kidnapped Pierre LaPorte, a Québec cabinet minister. Prime Minister Trudeau invoked the War Measures Act, which imposed emergency powers and allowed police to arrest people without laying charges. He also sent troops to Montréal, where they were instructed to assist police. Oops, there went equality and a just society. Well, for a time anyhow. The FLQ crisis ended within a few weeks. The terrorists executed Pierre LaPorte, but James Cross was released unharmed. Some of the terrorists received safe passage to Cuba, which also later kind of became a joke on them. Others were arrested, convicted and served prison sentences for kidnapping and murder.

The result of all of this fun and frolic in the '60s and the War Measures Act being imposed in 1970 was a larger non-violent separatist movement in Québec. Separatism had been building big time throughout the 1960s, but after the detention of so many innocents during the crisis, the separatist movement exploded—metaphorically speaking. By 1976, the separatist Parti Québecois, led by René Lévesque (you should know his name), was elected in Québec. In 1980, the province held its first referendum on separation from Canada. The bid was defeated and Canadians went back to their complacency, thinking phew, thank God that's over. But it wasn't.

Darkness Descends and Politicians Sing… This Is No Joke, Eh!

As the Trudeau era wound down, the Mulroney era began. It all started out all fine and dandy, but the end was cataclysmic for Canada. Okay, it wasn't cataclysmic, but it wasn't good, either. I am probably the only person that will ever admit this, and I am saddened by my mistake, but I voted for Mulroney and his PC party in their grand sweep of Parliament in 1984. You will be hard pressed, my friends, to find anyone else who will admit to this, though somehow the man and his party managed to win the largest majority in Canadian history. A scant nine years later, his party would also see the largest drubbing of any party in Canadian history—and a well-deserved drubbing by anyone's yardstick!

The Mulroney years were characterized by the negotiation of a free trade agreement between Canada, your aspiring home, and the U.S. Those years are also remembered for the introduction of the hated, evil, despicable, awful, ridiculous, terrible, mean, stupid, put-upon-us-by-a-bunch-of-idiots GST. The GST is a tax—the Goods and Services Tax—that is charged on almost everything you buy in Canada, whether it's a product like a package of gum or a service like having a muffler put on your car. This "fair" seven percent (now six percent) tax, as the Mulroney camp boneheads tried to pass it off, was what eventually did them in. Mulroney recently blamed his party's poor showing in the 1994 election on his female successor, Kim Campbell. But we all know it had nothing to do with her. It was all about him, and the only way the rest of us could get back at him was to absolutely decimate his party in an election. So we did.

Of course, Mulroney didn't care. He still had his ridiculously oversized Dudley Do-Right chin, his arrogance and his desire to go and start a boy band with his singing buddy, Ronald Reagan. You may or may not remember this, my American (soon to be fake Canadian) friends, but Mulroney and President Reagan met in 1985 at Québec City for what was referred to as the Shamrock Summit. It was called that because both of the chuckleheads had Irish backgrounds. The most famous moment of the summit was when Mulroney and Reagan performed a duet of "When Irish Eyes Are Smiling." I believe the answer to their refrain was, "The Devil Is Rubbing His Cloven Hooves Together."

PRIME MINISTER KIM CAMPBELL

And the Rest…Here on Canada's Isle!

The '90s saw the rather dull yet fiscally responsible governments of Liberal Jean Chrétien. Chrétien's time as prime minister started off in a way that was anything but dull. Because of inept meddling over the Canadian Constitution by the previous government, Québec had been left with more than a bad taste in her mouth. The result was that in 1995, Québec held a second referendum on separation from Canada. Although the separatist forces were defeated, the margin—50.58 percent against separation, 49.42 percent for—was so narrow that it left the country pretty much quaking in its mukluks. The separatist leader, Jacques Parizeau, kind of shot himself and his cause in the foot when after the defeat he blamed the loss on "money and the ethnic vote." Oops! Sure, he was disappointed, but there was no reason to go all Mel Gibson on the whole thing. Support for separation has declined since then.

In 1999, Nunavut became our third territory, bringing our total number of divisions to 13 (see The Thirteen). Mr. Chrétien also kept us out of the Gulf War Part Two, which is proving ever more to be a smart decision.

Mr. Chrétien is not a prime minister without controversy though. After the very close referendum on Québec sovereignty in 1995, the federal government set up a sponsorship program to raise awareness of its contribution to Québec industry. The program blew up in Chrétien's face when it was revealed that money earmarked for the program was being awarded in less-than-aboveboard ways. The resulting Sponsorship Scandal really only broke after Chrétien left office. His successor, Paul Martin, was left to try and deal with the mess. He set up a royal commission, the Gomery Commission, to investigate the wrongdoings and make recommendations. The result of all of it was that Martin, who tried to clean up the problem, was turfed from office, and Stephen Harper's minority Conservative government came to power largely by waving the banner of non-corruption.

Paul Martin should not be thought of as just a footnote in Canadian history, though. He is the man who, as Finance Minister under Chrétien, wrestled the deficit into control and was responsible for the all the surpluses Canada saw in recent years. As prime minister, Martin was thought to be indecisive, although I believe he was actually just a thinking man who wanted to do the right thing. Martin's major contribution as Prime Minister is probably having same-sex marriage legalized by passing a law in Parliament.

As for the same-sex marriage legislation, Harper and his neo-Conservative ideologues and his prim and proper church-lady type constituents and perhaps even his wives, I mean wife (of course, he only has one wife) tried to have the debate on same-sex marriage reopened by parliament. But parliament said, "No-way man! Asked and answered. Move on!" Besides, same-sex marriage has been passed into law by virtually every province and territory in the country. If Harper's government had reversed the law federally, it may have played to his Bible-challenged readers, but it would have had absolutely no effect on the country, except to have caused a really messy legal quagmire. Dodged a bullet on that one, Stephey-babe!

So, what lies ahead? Well, the country is currently involved in a struggle to understand our involvement in the war in Afghanistan. One Canadian diplomat and 44 of our soldiers (and sadly counting at press time) have been killed there, and the latest polls suggest the country does not have confidence in the mission. The new Conservative government claims it is a black and white issue, and Canada must remain in Afghanistan. We may need to remain, but many Canadians are concerned that there doesn't seem to be a plan or an end to the mission.

As for other things ahead, who the heck knows really? But I'd say more history, mystery and political shenanigans. It's really the shenanigans of all sorts that I'm looking forward to…and so should you!

CHAPTER SIX

CULTURAL MOSAIC OR MELTING POT?
I Don't Know, but I'm Sure there's a Government Grant in it Somewhere...

The United States is often held up as a great melting pot of a nation...which of course explains the slime you see boiling over in Washington. Canada has at times been called a cultural mosaic or a multicultural country, which might imply that we can't make up our minds about what it is. Okay, there is some truth to that. But do immigrants shed their language and culture when they join this, their new land, and melt into one society or does everyone just have it their own way in an amazing hodgepodge of cultural and linguistic messiness? Which is true or which is false, right or wrong, best or worst? And what other contrasts could I use in a questioning tone and sentence structure like this? What other contrasts, indeed? That's a good one. Hey, will the real Canada please stand up!

There has been a great debate in this country since the 1960s over the whole mosaic, melting pot, multicultural issue. Well, okay, it's not really a great debate. It's more just a debate because, generally speaking, most people are bored by it, or when it's brought up, they say, "Mosaipoturalism? That's what happened to those poor people in Walkerton because the Mike Harris Tories decided that clean water didn't matter, right?" But, of course they'd be wrong. Not about the Mike Harris Tories, but about mosaipoturalism. No, really!

Canada being an ideal place of enlightenment of the highest order means that a patchwork quilt of ethnic groups, cultures and languages (as well as overly colourful patchwork quilts) co-exist harmoniously within a cultural mosaic of many colours. The country is a bit like Joseph and his coat of many colours, or

Amazing Technicolour Dreamcoat, as Andrew Lloyd Webber called it. But, of course, let's not forget what happened to Joseph after he wore that coat of many colours and was a big show-off about it. His jealous half-brothers sold him into bondage. Although we're not sure whether Joseph was into bondage or not, in the end, we all had to put up with Donny Osmond resurrecting his career by playing a half-naked and, yes, badly-needing-to-join-a-gym version of Joseph on stage.

So, the moral of the story is that even if Canada was a cultural mosaic/Technicolour Dreamcoat/multicultural society, we wouldn't show off about it, because we know that our jealous older half-brothers—not America or Britain, of course not either of you—would sell us into bondage.

So, where does that leave you, my Aspiring Reasonable Facsimile of a Canadian? Up a birch tree without snowshoes, I suppose. However, the answer to the melting pot or mosaic quandary probably lies somewhere in this direction: It doesn't really matter, because I love ethnic food, and now because of all this mixing of different cultures, I get to eat it! And where I grew up— Hamilton, as I'm sure you remember—black pepper was considered ethnic. Sad, but true!

This may all seem simplistic in its structure and reasoning, but it couldn't ever be as bad as either a melting pot or a mosaic/multiculturalism explanation.

But if you continue the debate, there is most likely a government grant in it for you. That is no joke, right government granting body? Could I have my money now? I talked about the mosaic and the melting pot. I believe I've said enough now, except that you should eat ethnic!

Then there's the Whole Issue of Privilege...

Privilege is a whole other issue on the Canadian landscape—it's larger than a Rocky mountain, though it tries to be smaller than a debutante's pimple—and it is related to the cultural mosaic. Basically, privilege nullifies all the levelling effects that official multiculturalism pretends to favour. Let's have Bobo and Bitsy Gotsalot von Keepinit explain in an overheard (and made-up) conversation:

Bobo: Oh, look luvvy, if we throw them this little bone here, the hoi polloi, unwashed masses, ethnics, Hamiltonians and the like will stop suggesting we wealthy and elitist snobs get all the perks. While at the same time, we will retain all the important perks.

Bitsy: And make ourselves feel really, really good in the process.

Bobo: And don't forget superior.

Bitsy: Oh, no, no, one mustn't, nay can't, forget our obvious superiority.

Bobo: Oh, rah-thur.

Bitsy: Uh, honh, honh. (Privileged laughing)

Bobo: Well, that's a good day's work done.

Bitsy: Oh, yes indeed.

Bobo: I think I'll go do some heavy petting with the cat now, if you know what I mean.

Bitsy: Rah-thur. And I'll take these rather delightful and delusion-inducing medications.

Bobo: Enjoy!

Bitsy: Oh, and you too, enjoy dear. Enjoy!

In the United States, it is often said that someone can come from humble beginnings and grow up to be president. I'm pretty sure that's not true. George Bush, father and son, did not come from humble beginnings. They have no idea what the word humble means, and no, its not because they couldn't afford to buy a dictionary. Bill Clinton does appear to have come from humble roots; however, your elite got him for daring to dream that he could raise himself above his allotted station in life. And got him good they did, with the most tawdry, demeaning and absolutely irrelevant issue to his being president. In Canada, I know that this cannot happen. To be prime minister, one must come from money and privilege.

Our former Governor General, Adrienne Clarkson, recently published her memoirs and that prompts my riff on privilege. Oh, my goodness, what a life she's had. I mean she's been through the wringer. That is, if a wringer was having her nails done each morning by personal servants who she now can't beat because times have changed. Her servants did her time in the wringer, so she at least knows what it's like to have to drown out the sounds of suffering.

The former GG talks about the hardships she endured coming from a family of privilege in Hong Kong and then moving to God-forsaken Ottawa. (Oh, my God, I'm in tears. I don't think I can go on. But I must.) She and her family maintained their regal air, hoity-toity attitude and privilege in Ottawa. (In Ottawa? Oh, so, so sad!) Then the horrors she suffered attending Trinity College at the University of Toronto. (She had to wear plaid!) All the hard work she did in TV at the CBC. (She once had to sharpen her own pencil and only had seven big-haired girls and a fag from Moncton to do her hair and makeup!) And worst of all, becoming Governor General and having to sit through the Queen

powdering her nose during a formal dinner and the Queen Mum serving her stale cookies on mismatched china. (Oh, the inhumanity! The woman has suffered hardship upon hardship upon hardship.)

Cue the music: "Don't Cry for Me, Argentina"

We weep for you, Adrienne Clarkson.
The truth is you never suffered,
All through your privileged days,
Your tax-free existence,
You fulfilled your promise
Now keep your distance.

NEXT!

There would be nothing wrong with these privileged few going about their privileged existence if they'd just be quiet about it. Yet when they get some spotlight, they don't want to share it—and they certainly don't want to fade away into the background. No sirree, the limelight is where they shine! I mean, look at what Madam Clarkson did for this country. Truly an inspiration! She and her husband—and a royal entourage of some 7000 persons, give or take a few—took a government-sponsored trip through the Arctic, bringing her regal, Governor-General-like ways to the happy Inuit, who she patted on the head and told, "There, there. I'm here for you." Then she got back on her plane, sipped her martini and the Inuit were left to ponder. Picture an Arctic community, windswept and dotted with broken-down trailers:

Phil: Who was that lady?

Kenny: That was no lady. That was the Governor General.

Phil: Really? So, what was she doing here?

Kenny: No one knows. She did say, "There, there."

Phil: Oh, we must have signed a new treaty. I wonder what they stole from us this time?

Kenny: Don't know. Probably more ice. They need it for their drinks. We gave her the tarp that was covering Matt's old, broken skidoo.

Phil: The one with the vomit on it?

Kenny: Yeah, well, we didn't know she was coming and we had to give her something. We told her it was painted with a tradi-tional Inuit scene. I said "polar bear in a vomitorium" in Inuktitut. She didn't get it, but we all laughed anyways.

Phil: Did she bring us anything to eat?

Kenny: Same as usual…Hmm?

Phil: Hmm.

Kenny: Snow soup again, then, eh?

Phil: Oh, yeah.

So the Inuit and the rest of us hoi polloi are certainly better off because Adrienne Clarkson was our Governor General. What an inspiration! And I'd have stuck with that fake, yet polite inspirational line if she'd just go away. But she won't. She's now out hawking a book trying to show how her former boss in London—the Queen—is less mannered than she herself, the Clarkson woman. One cannot help but think that by suggesting someone else doesn't have manners or class, one reveals one's own lack of class, though you didn't hear that from me.

But for you, well-meaning soon-to-be fake Canadians, all you have to remember is that you don't come from privilege, so you'll never be in a position of privilege in Canada—unless you are that former president looking for a new homeland in which to reside because you screwed things up so badly in your two terms as "The Decider." In your case, your days of privilege are over too, although, I'll bet Adrienne Clarkson would love to be your friend. Maybe there's a photo-op in it for both of you.

Then There's the Compassionate Society

The measure of a society is how it takes care of its most vulnerable. Except for Conservative governments that are always saying "less tax" and "every man for himself," socialism exists in Canada and does ensure that our country's most vulnerable are taken care of. There are lapses and gaps, and sometimes things fall through the cracks, but generally speaking, it works. Canadians also like it this way.

Like many Canadians, I was brought up to believe that people should not be abandoned in their hour of need. That is the point of government and why we come together as a people—because we are stronger as a group than as one. Medicare, prescription drug assistance, old age pensions, employment insurance, childcare benefits, even respect for judges (despite being lawyers) are all hallmarks of Canadian society. There's really nothing funny to be said about it. Just remember that this is the type of civilized society you are looking to join. So don't come here and insist lower taxes are the only way to go. With lower taxes, we have learned, people suffer and die. That is not Canadian, and you wouldn't want to give yourselves away, now would you?

More important is where that tax money is going. Liberal governments have done a much better job of taking care of us—Conservative governments not so much. Thankfully, Conservative governments never last that long because they are out for the individual, which means themselves, and who the hell likes a haughty Conservative who's full of himself?

CHAPTER SEVEN

THE MYTH OF CANADIAN POLITENESS…SORRY ABOUT THIS, REALLY!

Canadians are nothing, if not polite, right? That's the way we're viewed in the world, and it's the way we view ourselves. However, it isn't true. Well, the fact that it isn't true isn't entirely true either. It's like a double negative, which ends up being positive. What I mean by all this is that we Canadians are polite, but that's not the only thing going on.

It's all just a surface thing. A camouflage. A smokescreen. Sorry, it's not all that, but it is some of that. No really, I wouldn't *steer* you wrong—unless you stuck me way back in *steer*age and thought I wouldn't mind because "Oh, the Canadians never mind such things."

On the surface, without getting to know us, you will think we are polite. That is the image we project. Having lived in the United States, I know that Americans like to accept a surface image. It doesn't clog their minds or require deep thinking or any particular thinking at all. It's easy:

"Hey hon. Look at the Canadians. They're so nice."

"Yeah, nice."

"Nice…"

"…Nice…Wanna steal from them now?"

And that makes it easy for us to fool Americans into thinking we're polite, because we are, at least on the surface. But we're not really. Evolution, survival of the fittest and simply living next to the U.S. has made us this way. It's all about self-preservation. Look elsewhere in this book for the War of 1812 or the Alaska Boundary Dispute or a myriad of other things that have happened in our history, and you will see they have taught us to appear benign and polite, even if we're not.

This trickles down from a national level to a personal one. We use politeness to ensure that people don't know our true nature. Not because we are evil, awful or bad, though to be fair I have to admit some of us are, but because we are secretive. We don't like people keeping tabs on us, so we don't draw attention to ourselves. This all fits in with the Essence of Being Canadian, so if you've forgotten that, you might want to go back and read it again for real this time.

If someone mistakenly brushes against us while we are riding on a bus, the rush will be on to see who can say "sorry" first, no matter who did the initial brushing. And the reason for this is so that we are not judged. If both parties say "sorry," both will then go about their day not thinking again of the incident or the person. If the same thing happens, and one person says "sorry" and the other doesn't, for the rest of the day the polite one will think the other person is someone who could be best described by a compound slang word derived from the back end of a human or animal plus the results of a ditch digger's work. In fact, if a "sorry" isn't forthcoming, the polite one may even utter an unpleasant word under his breath.

What is this all about? What is the sense in all this? Well, it's because we are a nation of judgers. We say "sorry" whether someone is hurt or not, to avoid being judged. So the polite exterior really just masks a really hypersensitive and judgmental interior. If you do not hold a door open for us, you will be judged. If you slightly brush up against us and do not acknowledge it, you will be judged. If you have sex with our

marital partner without asking, you will be judged. For that, you will really be judged!

This politeness extends even farther with some of us and allows us to gauge how much we can, should or will reveal about ourselves with others. We are quite happy to be self-deprecating. We are also happy to allow others to join in with us, as long as they are one of us. However, if we appear self-deprecating, and then you, who have just met us, join in mocking us, you're dead in the water. For again, we make a mental note: "You are a self-centred jerk, who overestimates his importance and could be best described by a compound slang word derived from the back end of a human or animal plus the results of a ditch digger's work."

The correct response in a new situation where someone is being self-deprecating is to not join in mocking him, but instead begin mocking yourself. Others will join the self-mockfest until we are all one-upping each other in a joyous and disturbingly strange festival of self-mockery:

"No way, eh. I'm the bigger hoser!"

"Yeah, well, I'm from Alberta!"

This says, "Hey, we're all equal, all the same." It does not say, "Hey, what a big stupid goof you are. Let me pile on and mock you, too, person I've just met." I mean, that's impolite and untoward, and well, we'll get you for it.

Our big festival of self-mockery is called Oktoberfest, which takes place during Oktober, which is the same as October, but happens only once every six years because the sixth year of Oktober naturally calls all mockers and mocked home for the mocking. If you understand this, you've either been mocked or have gotten the call.

All of this politeness (or not) may seem unimportant, stupid, or silly even. But beware of the politeness that is Canadian, for it masks a wicked, astute and immediately judgmental, ah, judger. So feel free to judge, but judge quietly, for you will also be judged! No really. And I'm really sorry about that. Really.

CHAPTER EIGHT

CANADIAN WORDS LIKE "EH!"

One thing Americans and most people around the world don't know about Canada and Canadians is that we have a completely unique and distinct language. Most people who aren't dimwits recognize that we have two official languages—English and French—or at least eventually figure that out. However, now I will reveal to you something about language in Canada that only real Canadians know and we have all taken an oath to uphold and keep secret. Psst, okay now, you must keep this under your hat and never let anyone know that you know this or where you learned of it.

Canada has two official languages, but only one real language. It is a difficult language to learn, takes years of practice to master, and one can only truly be proficient in it if guided by a real Canadian language guru, known as "desoh neeb tsuj evah uoy." To read the official name of a real Canadian language guru, or for that matter, anything in the real Canadian language, you must read from right to left instead of the traditional left to right construction used in most Western languages. I'll wait for you to go back and read the name now...

That's Right, I've just Pulled the Proverbial Snow over your Parka!

There isn't, in fact, a distinctly Canadian language, though I'm here now to highlight some of the glaring differences between Canadian usage and the rest of the world. Both Canadian English and French borrow from British English and American English, and that is of course how you end up with "le hotdog" in French Canadian, which means wiener dog or dachshund. Not really. It actually means hotdog, as in frankfurter. I am not going to deal further with the French side of things, since I am far from an expert, and I am aiming this helpful piece of Can-lit at an American English-speaking market. I'm sorry, but those Americans who speak other languages, whether Spanish or Swahili, you're going to at least have to convert to English to get any value out of this book at all—that is, unless you're using it for kindling or toilet paper. If you are using it for those purposes, go ahead, light or wipe away! As for the rest, here goes.

Rule # 1

The first thing you should assume, and I can't believe I am writing this, is that if I haven't pointed out a difference, it is probably spelled the same and/or pronounced the same in Canadian and American English.

Rule # 2: –our and –re

One of the biggest differences is the way we spell things. If you don't intend to write much of anything, which I advise for most people, you won't have to consider this very often. However, if you see signs that you think are spelled wrong and point them out, you might just reveal yourself as a non-Canadian. In Canada, we usually defer to British spellings rather than to the often-shorter American English versions. Many words derived from French end in "–or" and "–er" in American English, but in Canadian English end in "–our" and "–re." The best examples of these are colour, honour and neighbour for the "–our" words and centre and metre for the" –re" words.

Rule # 3: Cheque

One glaring difference in terms of a word that is spelled differently in Canada than it is in America is the word "cheque." In the United States, they write it "check." Both words are pronounced the same; however, in Canada we write a cheque to pay a bill, but we will check to see if something is in stock. This is one of those mistakes that will give you away as an American.

Rule # 4: Pronunciation

When in doubt pronounce it like an American, but remember these differences:

Asphalt: the strange Canadian pronunciation is *ash-fault*

Fragile, fertile and mobile: they are pronounced with an emphasis on the "-ile" part, and the "-ile" is pronounced like *aisle*

Out and about: these are the two words that apparently give Canadians away to Americans. They are really pronounced with a nasal sort of twang, and the closest written representation I can come up with is *owt* and *uhbowt*.

Premier: the leader of each province is called the premier and is pronounced *pree-myur* or *pree-meer*

Premiere: the first showing of a film is called the premiere and is pronounced *prem-yair*

Toronto: pronounced *Tuhrana* or *Trana*. No second "t" in either.

Z: the last letter of the alphabet is called "zed" and rhymes with "bed" in Canada. You can say "zee" and be understood, but you'll also get funny looks.

Rule # 5: Education-Related Giveaways

Students always talk about their grade level in terms of grade one, grade two, grade ten and grade twelve. We never say first grade or tenth grade.

In Canada, we don't use the term "college" to describe all post-secondary institutions. College is used to describe community colleges or technical schools. "University" describes, well, universities. At a university, first-year students are often referred to as frosh. However, in Canada we don't use the terms freshmen, sophomore, junior or senior either in high school or university. In university, students are frosh/first year, second year, third year or fourth year.

More Words at Random

Acadian

It's Not: a mispronunciation of the phrase "a Canadian"

It Is (The Short Answer): people who got hosed when the French lost their Canadian colonies

It Is (The Long Answer): the original French colony in North America was called Acadia and encompassed everything from the Atlantic Ocean to the St. Lawrence, meaning Nova Scotia, New Brunswick, Prince Edward Island, southeastern Québec and even part of Maine. When the French-English battles over North America were finally settled, the French got booted and the English decided they couldn't trust anyone who didn't swear an oath of allegiance to Britain. The Acadians were dispersed all over North America, and the best-known group of these settled in Louisiana, where their descendants became known as Cajuns and eventually were hosed when Hurricane Katrina hit that state.

Alberta Clipper

It's Not: a type of landscaping device that is used in Alberta to form mountains into mole hills

It Is: a big blowhard. It's not associated with a politician, but it blows across the plains of North America bringing frigid temperatures, disdain from Americans and a whole lot of windy weather.

Albertosaurus

It's Not: a person from Alberta with old fashioned, staid or even dinosaur-like ideas

It Is: a big dinosaur resembling the Tyrannosaurus Rex but slightly smaller. The remains of Albertosaurus were originally discovered in 1884 in the province of Alberta by Joseph Tyrrell in an area called the Badlands, not because they are rebellious, but because they're generally inhospitable. Don't you hate it when geographical areas don't have manners?

ABM or ATM

It's Not: an automated bagel machine or automated tomato machine. Neither dispenses food items

It Is: a bank machine, as in a machine that dispenses money. They are also sometimes called instant tellers.

Allophone

It's Not: a telephone that automatically answers in French, saying "Allo?"

It Is: a person living in the province of Québec whose native language is neither English nor French

Bachelor

It's Not: a French term for the groupies of a 17th-century German composer

It Is: a small, one-room apartment, as in: "Are you looking to rent a bachelor or a one-bedroom?"

Canadian Tire Money

It's Not: the currency of the realm

It Is: cash bonus coupons awarded in the amount of five percent on cash purchases at all Canadian Tire stores and redeemable on purchases at the retailer. Say what? Canadian Tire is a department store founded in Toronto by two brothers, John and Alfred Billes, in the 1920s. The brothers started out stocking car parts. Since then, Canadian Tire has expanded to every part of Canada. Now Canadian Tire is a place to get your car repaired and shop for car parts of all makes and models as well as sporting goods, tools, hardware and home and leisure items. Today, 90 percent of Canadians shop at Canadian Tire at least twice a year, and 40 percent shop at the store every week.

Can-con

It's not: the Canadian version of a French dance where the ladies show their naughty bits

It Is: a shortened form of "Canadian content." Can-con refers to a percentage of content (songs, TV programs, films) that must be aired by Canadian broadcasters.

It's not, but it could be: a Canadian con man who is subsidized by taxpayers and has the official title of prime minister, cabinet minister or politician.

Can-Lit

It's not: a way to make an aluminum soda can glow by lighting it on fire and turning it into a Canadian version of a Molotov cocktail for use in riots. If it were, it would be used rarely since riots are almost non-existent in the Great White North… because it's too cold.

It is: a shortened form of Canadian literature, and when I say Canadian literature, I mean the kind that's serious and good for you and that civil servants who run government granting bodies feel really good about because they've funded it. In other words, it is literature that wouldn't exist if it weren't for subsidies. Establishment elites have adopted this term, which was originally used as a mocking title to describe the literature that they consider "very important." You know, the kind of stuff nobody actually reads. This book, for instance, would never be mistaken for Can-Lit despite being written by a Canadian citizen and published by a Canadian publisher. Books by Margaret Atwood and others of her ilk are part of the Can-Lit lexicon.

Canuck

It's not: a mispronunciation of the word "knuck"

It is: a slang term for a Canadian as well as the name of the National Hockey League (NHL) team in Vancouver

Chinook

It's not: the Canadian spelling of a word of Yiddish origin meaning someone who is stupid or easily victimized (schnook)

It is: a big blowhard, or more accurately, a warm dry wind that swoops down the eastern slopes of the Rockies and can cause temperatures to rise by 20° Celsius

It's also: a type of salmon

Concession Road

It's not: a less desirable route of travel, as in: "We took the concession road, the first runner-up in terms of roads, because the main road was booked and used by more beautiful people, and quite frankly, it thought itself much too good for us."

It is: a term only used in Ontario and Québec to describe one of a set of roads originally laid out by the colonial government. I grew up in Hamilton, Ontario, just one block away from Concession Street, which was originally named Concession Road Number One.

Deke

It's Not: the way that French-Canadians pronounce a word for a male body part

It Is: a term used in sports, most often in hockey, to describe a quick move that fakes out an opponent

Dick All

It's Not: a term describing the activities of a promiscuous male

It Is: a rather crass slang term meaning "nothing." Question: "What are you doing today?" Response: "Dick all!"

Eavestrough

It's Not: a girl born in the gutter

It Is: something referred to as "gutters" by many Americans. They hang from the roofs of houses, catch rain and snow run-off and carry it to the ground. In Canada, gutters are a place where politicians do most of their business, as in "in the gutter."

Eh

It's Not: the most commonly used word in the Canadian vocabulary, although it is a close second or third

It Is: a word used at the end of a sentence with the purpose of turning a statement into a rhetorical question…and, of course, making the person using the construction sound like a "hoser"

René: Canada sure is a wonderful place to live despite the cold, the blackflies, the bad television programming and acid rain, eh?

Pierre: Oh yeah, eh?

René: Eh, eh?

Pierre: Eh?

Elastics
It's Not: a kitschy name for a rock band or comedy troupe

They Are: rubber bands

Foyer
It's Not: something you throw a log on and sit around to keep warm at camp

It Is: the entranceway of a house or open hall in a theatre, pronounced *foy-eh*, not *foy-ur*

Girl Guides
It's Not: a secret paramilitary organization that recruits girls and indoctrinates them in a religious-like fashion, teaching them to be self-sufficient and how to build campfires

It Is: a non-secret, non-paramilitary organization that recruits girls and indoctrinates them—giving them self-esteem while they live, grow, learn and contribute to their communities. The American equivalent would be the Girl Scouts.

Hosed
It's Not: something that is done to a woman to start a wet T-shirt contest

It Is: a term used by Bob and Doug McKenzie on *SCTV* and in their film *Strange Brew* that means "to be taken advantage of." A person who uses the term "hosed" is also referred to as the proverbial "hoser." Bob and Doug McKenzie are Canada's quintessential hoser kings.

Hydro
It's Not: water

It's Also Not: a male version of the Hydra, a monster from Greek mythology that had a serpent's body and many heads

It Is: a term Canadians often use interchangeably with electricity. Many Canadians will refer to their electric bill as their hydro bill. If the power goes out they will say the hydro is out. The word is a short form for hydroelectric power.

Jesus Murphy!

It's Not: what Canadians call Jesus Christ

It's Also Not: a homely guy who often pops up on CBC TV broadcasts with insightful commentaries

It Is: an exclamatory phrase that is interchangeable with "Goddamn!"

Language Police

It's Not: a fictional police force from an Orwellian novel that dictates the use of language in Canada

It Is: an actual Orwellian-like governmental body (Office de la Langue Française) in the province of Québec that dictates the use of the French language. The Language Police are charged with ensuring that businesses in the province of Québec use only French on signs and in the workplace. There have been various challenges and modifications to the original scope of the language law, but it still ensures that French is the main language used in Québec.

Loonie

It's Not: somebody who is really wacky. Okay, it is that too.

It Is More Commonly: the nickname for the dollar coin in Canada. It replaced the paper dollar bill in the late 1980s and has the Queen's head on one side. That's why it's called a loonie. Not really. It has a loon on

the other side, and that's why it's called a loonie.

Parkade

It's Not: a helpful parking lot attendant

It Is: a term used interchangeably with parking garage

Pogey

It's Not: Gumbie's pony pal

It Is: the social benefit paid to people who are unemployed. It's now more commonly referred to as U.I. (for unemployment insurance) or E.I. (for employment Insurance). The government changed the term from U.I. to E.I a few years back because it thought, in its infinite wisdom, that Employment Insurance was a more positive term than Unemployment Insurance.

Postal Code

It's Not: a system that warns people when a frustrated employee is going to go on a violent rampage. As in, "That guys going to go postal! Better send out the code."

It Is: the Canadian equivalent of an American zip code. It contains six alphanumeric characters with a space after the third one, in this form: M4Y 1L6.

Seat Sale

It's Not: an auction at a brothel

It Is: a reduced or special ticket price for travel by plane or sometimes by bus

Separate Schools

It's Not: French schools that teach the fine art of separating from Canada or at least threatening to do so every 10 years

It Is: school boards that are not part of the main public school system (but aren't private schools). In Ontario, they are most often associated with Catholic schools, although there are other types, not all of which are religiously based.

Snowbird

It's Not: an ice or snow sculpture in the form of a person's hand and finger "flipping the bird"

It Is: one of the many Canadians who reside in the southern United States during the winter months. It most often refers to senior citizens or retired folks like my parents.

It Is Also: a schmaltzy, but popular song by the famous Canadian singer Anne Murray

It Is Also Also: the name of the Canadian military's precision aerobatic team. The Snowbirds (431 Squadron) fly CT-114 Tutor Jets. They are similar to the U.S. air force's Blue Angels.

SIN
It's Not: something blasphemous as categorized by the Roman Catholic Church. That is spelled "s-i-n."

It Is: a social insurance number, the Canadian equivalent of the American social security number. It has nine numbers, just like the social security number, but it is written in a different form, like this: 123 456 789.

Take Off
It's Not: something done by an airplane…well, actually it is

It Is Also: a slang term meaning "get lost" or "screw off." The term was popularized by the characters Bob and Doug McKenzie (played by Rick Moranis and Dave Thomas)

on the comedy show *SCTV* and in the film *Strange Brew*, but Canadians don't use this expression…at least no Canadians that I know.

Tobaggan
It's Not: a recreational sport carried out like water-skiing, but in muddy bogs

It Is: a narrow sled that is curled up at one end. It's pronounced *tuh-bog-in*

Toonie
It's Not: the sister of Woody Allen's wife

It Is: The $2 coin in Canada that replaced the $2 paper bill in the 1990s. The toonie got its name only because it rhymes with loonie (the slang name given to the dollar coin). Toonies are slightly larger than loonies and are bimetallic, having an outer ring that is silver in colour and a centre that is copper coloured. The Queen's head is on one side of the toonie, and there's a polar bear on the other side.

Washroom
It's Not: a place where clothes are washed

It Is: what Canadians call a restroom. We also call it the men's room or ladies' room.

And Then There Are the Places You'll Need to Remember, Eh!

Lotus Land
It's Not: any place where wacky, drug-addled people live in a happy state of haziness while they constantly work at playing

It Is: a place where wacky, drug-addled people live in a happy state of haziness while they constantly work at playing. In other words, it's a colloquial term for British Columbia.

The Rock
It's Not: a town named after a wrestler-turned-Hollywood-actor

It Is: a colloquial term for Newfoundland

The Soo
It's Not: the one day a year when all of Canada's lawyers get together to try their cases. It's usually only a half-day

because we're still a small country and law abiding as well.

It Is: a short form for the city of Sault Ste. Marie, Ontario

Canadian Products You May or May Not Know

Arborite
It's Not: an annual festival of light, celebrating the tree.

It Is: a brand name that is now used to describe just about any crappy, cheap-looking laminated countertop. We actually have other good, nice and expensive countertops that do not go by the name of this cheap and tacky product.

Chesterfield
Its Not: a Mr. Field whose first name is Chester

It Is: originally, chesterfield was the name brand of a sofa or couch, but it is now used synonymously with those words

Javex
It's Not: the way people from the East Coast ask for "x," as in, "D'y'ave x?"

It Is: a name brand for bleach in Canada. However, it is interchangeably used just to mean bleach.

Kleenex
It's Not: the written form of the way Canadians pronounce "clinics"

It Is: a name brand of facial tissue in Canada. However, people almost never ask for a tissue, they will instead ask for Kleenex or a Kleenex.

CHAPTER NINE

IT'S ALL ABOUT THE FOOD, EH!

Just think for a second on all of the things you know about Canadian food. No, it's okay, keep thinking, I'll wait…

Lots of silence there, for sure! I do have to admit that Canada isn't really known for a style of food like the French or the Italians. We're more like Americans in that there really isn't a distinctly American cuisine beyond perhaps hamburgers and hotdogs, which we have as well. I know, I know, of late there are more and more star chefs and food TV shows that are trying to create American and Canadian cuisine, but mainly our two countries' culinary styles borrow from just about everywhere else. And we're just fine with that, aren't we?

What you'll notice about Canadian restaurant food is that portions tend to be smaller than those in restaurants in the United States. However, I'm pretty sure that portions are smaller just about everywhere as compared to the United States, except maybe Portugal. In Canada you also tend to get what you pay for, so a cheap meal is probably not going to be that good.

Service in restaurants is adequate, but not the same as you'll find in the United States either. In Toronto, for example, service is pretty bad, and that's mainly because waiters and waitresses are all aspiring actors, so they'd hate to commit themselves too much to the paying gig when they are really artistes.

There is perhaps one area in which Canadians excel, or at least take pride, in terms of food. It's a little odd and even slightly embarrassing, but it is a Canadian institution. And just what is that? Well, it's a little thing called Tim Hortons. Tim Horton was a Canadian hockey player who played defense for many seasons with the Toronto Maple Leafs. He also played with the

New York Rangers, Pittsburgh Penguins and, in his final years, with the Buffalo Sabres. He died in a car crash in 1974, but before his death he founded Tim Hortons. Yes, I know, I still have not given you the skinny on what exactly Tim Hortons, is. Well, my impatient, soon-to-be-doughnut-eating friends, Tim Hortons is a coffee and doughnut shop. Actually it's not just one store, although it did start out that way. In my home-town, Hamilton, Ontario, the first Tim Hortons set up shop on Ottawa Street in 1964. Today, there are 2600 Tim Hortons across Canada and 300 in the United States. Tim Hortons is so popular, in fact, that Canadian soldiers serving overseas often request care packages that include tins of Tim Hortons coffee.

So, there you have it, my Aspiring Reasonable Facsimile of a Canadian, Canada's dirty little secret when it comes to food is this: we're all about coffee and doughnuts. So if you are to fake your way into being one of us, head to your nearest Tim Hortons and you'll get a real sense of Canada. If you currently live in Connecticut, Massachusetts, Maine, Michigan, Kentucky, New York, Ohio, Pennsylvania, West Virginia or Rhode Island, you don't even have to leave your state to get a sense of us. Tim Hortons franchises exist in all of those states, and domination of the U.S. market is not far behind.

Timmy's Words

Tim Hortons is such an institution that there are a couple of words directly related to it:

Double-Double

It's Not: a deviant sexual term… although I suppose it could be

It Is: a way to order coffee with two creams and two sugars. As in, "I'll have a large double-double." The phrase may or may not have originated with Tim Hortons, but it is understood in every one of the franchises.

Timbits

It's Not: the cost of a shave and a haircut. "Shave and a haircut, Timbits!"

It Is: the equivalent of a donut hole. Instead of wasting the centres popped out of the doughnuts, Tim Hortons turned them into round, deep fried, sugary balls they call Timbits.

Other Canadian Food-Related Words, Eh…

Canadian Bacon

It's Not: something eaten by Canadians

It Is: a name used by Americans to describe what Canadians call "back bacon" in some parts of the country (in the west) and "thinly sliced rolled ham" (in Ontario). So, remember, if you do not want to give yourself away as an American, never ask for Canadian bacon. (See also "Peameal Bacon" below.)

Canola

It's Not: how Spanish-Canadians say hello

It Is: a modified member of the rapeseed family that Canadians have turned into an extremely healthy cooking oil

Chocolate Bar

It's Not: a seedy drinking establishment that specializes in getting people drunk on chocolate and then shanghaiing them into forced labour in candy factories

It Is: the Canadian equivalent of the American term "candy bar"

Cutlery

It's Not: a threatening gesture used towards a man named Larry or Lery, as in "I'm gonna cut-lery"

It Is: silverware or flatware (as in knives, forks and spoons, for those who might be a little slow on the uptake)

Joe Louis Cakes
It's Not: the description of the rear end of a famous American boxer

It Is: a hand-sized, chocolate-covered chocolate cake that has a layer of vanilla icing sandwiched in its centre. These are extremely (some might say sickeningly) sweet, individually wrapped dessert cakes that are made in Québec and distributed throughout Canada. The cake was named after the sons of Arcade and Rose-Anna Vachon, the original makers of the cakes, not after the American boxer. The cake's name is also pronounced *joe-lew-ie.*

Kraft Dinner
It's Not: a meal prepared in the Arts and Crafts style or using crafty methods like decoupage

It Is: the name brand of the ubiquitous boxed macaroni-and-cheese meal produced by Kraft Foods in Canada. The box is navy blue with yellow lettering, and the contents include dry macaroni and a single packet of dried cheese that has a distinctive day-glow orange-yellow colouring. In the United States, it is simply sold as Kraft Macaroni and Cheese. To make Kraft Dinner, one only has to boil the macaroni in the water, drain, add milk and butter and then stir in the cheese. Some Canadians have also been known to add sliced hotdogs to the Kraft Dinner to make it more…hearty. Remember to call it Kraft Dinner. However, macaroni and cheese not made from the boxed product is not referred to as Kraft Dinner. It is called macaroni and cheese. Well, duh!

Peameal Bacon
It's Not: a soggy meat product made from pigs and cured in Saskatchewan's famous yellow snow

It Is: a tasty cross between ham and bacon. Boneless pork loin was originally cured in pickle brine and then rolled in ground yellow peas. Cornmeal has replaced the peas in modern incarnations, but the name remains the same. I'm telling you. Try it, you'll like it!

Pop

It's not: how a weasel goes

It is: how Canadians refer to carbonated beverages, in the same way that Americans call them sodas. We also refer to them by name brands or varieties: Coke, Pepsi, ginger ale, root beer, etc…

Poutine

It's Not: an adolescent cartoon character that resembles a turd…as in Pooteen

It Is: french fries topped with cheese curd and then drowned in gravy. I am not a fan of this gooey mess that originated in Québec. As you can probably guess, French Canadian food does not have a lot in common with French cuisine from France.

Serviette

It's Not: the term used to describe a female server or waitress in Québec

It Is: a napkin

Smarties

It's Not: the secret code name we call ourselves, except in public where Canadian, Canuck or hoser is always used

It Is: the name brand of a candy-coated chocolate that resembles, although doesn't taste like, M&Ms. The plain kind. There are no chocolate-covered peanuts in the Smarties box.

Oh, and the Drinks, too, Eh! Or How to Drink Like a Canadian

From the list of words below, one would think that Canadians are some of the biggest alcoholics in the world. Well, we're not... at least I don't think we are. Statistics Canada agrees with me on this; however, I have been told by a businessman/politician/ crook that you can use statistics to prove absolutely any side of any argument you want to. Ahem...

We are mainly responsible drinkers as individuals and as a whole in Canada. Beer has always been the most popular of alcoholic beverages in Canada. Spirits (whiskey and the like) have been a prominent second, and wines have always brought up the rear. Though they are usually ingested from the front, except during fraternity hazing rituals. However, things have changed in the last few decades, and the latest statistics suggest that wine is now second to beer, though still ingested frontwise. So, there you go, we've become sophisticated wine drinkers as opposed to falling-down drunks like Sir John A. Macdonald, our first prime minister. Progress is a nifty thing!

Beer Store
It's Not: a retail outlet made of beer or floating on beer. Well, not exactly.

It Is: officially known as the Brewer's Retail. In Ontario, breweries have pooled their resources and set up outlets for consumers to buy their beer. You can get all different brands in all different sizes (see below) at the beer store. You can also buy beer in liquor stores in Ontario, but there isn't nearly the selection of brands or quantities.

Forty-pounder
It's Not: the weight of a standard-issue beer-bottle opener

It's Also Not: the term used to describe a drunk guy who wants to fight the entire bar

It Is: the slang term for a 40-ounce bottle of spirits (whiskey, rum, vodka, etc.). It is also referred to as a forty-ouncer.

Kokanee

It's Not: the act of balancing a can of Coke on one's knee for the purposes of winning a bar game

It Is: the name of a species of land-locked salmon found in British Columbia

It Is Also: a brand of beer originally produced in British Columbia but now distributed elsewhere in Canada

LCBO

It's Not: a rarely used acronym for the Lousy Cruddy Business Organization

It Is: what government-run liquor stores are called in Ontario. Ontarians use either "liquor store" or "LCBO" interchangeably. The LCBO runs more than 600 stores in Ontario and is one of the largest single purchasers of alcohol in the world. This means that a lot of foreign booze imported into Ontario is rather cheap to buy. Vive le LCBO! Many other parts of the country have a similar system. The big exception is in Alberta, where they privatized all the liquor stores and prices went up.

Those Albertans sure have some good ideas.

Mickey

It's Not: the name of a mouse with a high-pitched voice that fronts one of the most evil organizations known to man

It Is: a 13-ounce bottle of liquor that can conveniently fit into a pocket

Poverty Pack

It's Not: essentials given to the less fortunate to help tide them over until better times

It Is: a six-pack of beer, so designated because only the poverty stricken would buy beer in such a small quantity. At least that's the derogatory way the term is used.

Screech

It's Not: the sound that René Lévesque's brakes made when he ran over that guy. You know the one I mean. You need to know that René Lévesque was the Premier of the province of Quebec, and the incident I refer to can be found on the net. Glug, glug, vroom, vroom, bump, bump, if you know what I mean.

It Is: a potent, almost gasoline-like rum produced in Newfoundland. Every Canadian has probably had a taste of screech at some time during his life. If one is not a Newfoundlander, life tends to end immediately following more than just a taste.

Twenty-sixer
It's Not: a 26-pack of beer. Twenty-six beers in one pack would just be wrong!

It Is: a 26-ounce bottle of spirits

Two-four

It's Not: the way small policemen acknowledge receipt of a radio message

It Is: a case of 24 bottles of beer. This is the standard quantity for Canadians to purchase beer. It can be pronounced *two-four* or *two-fur*.

CHAPTER TEN

THE YARDSTICK IS A BIT LONGER UP HERE... THAT'S BECAUSE IT'S A METRE

Another thing that will make the transition from American to Reasonable Facsimile of a Canadian more difficult is the way we measure everything in Canada, except time. That is still measured in seconds, minutes, hours, days, weeks, months, years, decades, centuries and millennia, although I personally have not lived for an entire millennium or longer, as you have already probably guessed. That is, unless you thought perhaps my vast knowledge of Canada makes me a lumber-jacket-wearing wizard of monumental abilities and brains who has an ultra-long lifespan and the ability to travel through time while tracking down and slaying demons in a gravity-defying, Steven Spielberg way. Of course, I never wear lumber jackets. I also cannot travel through time in any way that makes me more special than your typical Canadian human being. But thanks for the high praise and the somewhat nifty scenario.

I have been alive for a generation, an indict and half, and an Olympiad (approximately). You could also say that I have lived for two score and two years, if that measurement is somewhat easier for you. One other way to measure my life span so far would be eight lustrum and two. Go look those up, because they are real measurements of time, although a couple of them are somewhat obsolete. You can view this research assignment as a form of homework, and thus this book will seem more like a serious instructional guide. Okay, away you go!

Now let me turn to the information you are so desperately in need of and for which this section was so ingeniously titled.

Measurements in Canada—weather measurement, speed, speed limits, distance, weight, volume and dimensions—are generally done using a different system of measure than in the U.S. In fact, 99 percent of the world uses the same system that Canadians were forced to adopt in the 1970s: the metric system. I specify that we were forced to adopt the metric system because it was imposed on us by the Trudeau Liberals, and although one would have to admit it was the right way to go, we didn't take kindly to being forced. Who likes a pushy government, right? However, we have mostly learned to use the metric system, except for those people of a certain generation and older. The generation I am referring to is my own. So if you are 40 or older and don't understand or comprehend a measurement given in Canada, just wrinkle up your nose and say "What's that in non-metric?" You could also use the terms "imperial units," "real numbers" or "the old way" interchangeably with the phrase "non-metric."

The two main areas where metric really hasn't taken over Canadian society are in measurements of our bodies and in the kitchen. We still measure our bodies using pounds, feet and inches and recipes using tablespoons, teaspoons and cups. Why? I have no idea, but it'll make it slightly easier on you so don't question it. Although I do have a theory on why Americans haven't adopted the metric system: the French invented it. Enough said, right?

Here are some handy-dandy details on metric that you'll need to know and some additional and helpful ways to convert them to "American" measures so you can understand them.

The Sense that Metric Makes, Although I Am Hardly an Advocate...

The metric system is a decimalized system of measure. What that means is there are basic units of measure and everything else is either a multiple or decimal of the basic units. The basic units in metric are the metre for length, width or distance; the gram for weight; the litre for volume; and degrees Celsius for temperature. The best way to think of the metric system is in terms of your money, which is already metric—Canadian and American money. Say what? It's true. The dollar is the basic unit of money, right? If you want smaller denominations (or units) of money, you're talking cents, although wanting cents as opposed to dollars doesn't make much sense. There are 100 cents in a dollar. That's metric. The standard measure of length or width is the metre. A metre is just over the length of a yard—39 inches. Within a metre, you will find 100 centimetres. Remember, 100 cents make up a dollar? Well, 100 centimetres make up a metre. It's the same with volume and weight measures, except that they use the litre or gram as their standard unit of measure.

The names of multiples or sub-multiples of standard units are formed by using prefixes. One one-hundredth of a metre is a centimeter—that's a sub-multiple formed by adding centi- to metre. One thousand metres is a kilometer—a multiple

formed by adding kilo- to metre. The standard prefixes include the following, but not all of them are in wide use: deca- (ten), hecto- (hundred), kilo- (thousand), mega- (million), giga- (billion); deci- (tenth), centi- (hundredth), milli- (thousandth), micro- (millionth) and nano- (billionth). You have probably heard some or all of these if you've ever seen anything at all to do with *Star Trek*.

Temperature's a Bit of an Oddity

The only variation on the whole prefix issue is in terms of temperature, where everything is just measured in degrees Celsius. Water boils at 100° Celsius and freezes at 0° Celsius. Anything less than 0° Celsius is expressed with a minus sign. So, 28° Fahrenheit is –2° degrees Celsius. Many Canadians still talk about temperature in terms of degrees Fahrenheit, though officially we're not supposed to. I think it's a law. Like that would ever stop us. You didn't hear that from me.

For the Handymen Among You

Length and width of rooms, windows, picture frames and other such things can still be done using good old inches and feet. However, if you want to look all mod, go for the metric measure. If you're using a tape measure, you're in luck because most of them have both metric and imperial units.

Driving and Speed

Driving distances are always measured in kilometres, and speed is measured in kilometres per hour. Highway speed limits are usually 100 kilometres per hour maximum. If someone wants to know the "mileage" on a car, they will actually ask for the mileage, although the answer is given in kilometers.

"How many miles on that car, Bill?"

"Sixty thousand kilometers." Or "Sixty thousand klicks".

Converting

Centimetres and Inches
1 inch = 2.54 centimetres
1 centimetre = .39 inches

Metres and Feet
1 metre = 3.28 feet
1 foot = .30 metres

Kilometres and Miles
1 kilometre = 0.62 miles
1 mile = 1.61 kilometres

Kilos and Pounds
1 kilogram = 2.20 pounds
1 pound = 0.45 kilograms

Litres and Gallons

Gasoline is measured in litres, and vehicle consumption of gasoline is measured in kilometers to the litre. For the purposes of this conversion, we are talking about U.S. gallons, not U.K. gallons.

1 litre = 0.26 gallons
1 gallon = 3.79 litres

Millilitres and Ounces

For the purposes of this conversion, we are talking about U.S. ounces, not U.K. ounces.

1 millilitre = 0.03 ounces
1 ounce = 29.57 millilitres

Temperature

Multiply the Celsius temperature by $9/5$ and add 32.

25° Celsius = (25 x $9/5$ + 32) 77° Fahrenheit
0° Celsius = 32° Fahrenheit
10° Celsius = 50° Fahrenheit
20° Celsius = 68° Fahrenheit
30° Celsius = 86° Fahrenheit
40° Celsius = 104° Fahrenheit

A Note on Canadian Money

That's right, we've taken to using money in Canada because the whole honour system stopped working. The honour system, or *system d'honeur* in Québec, lasted a good 150 years or so, but then some unscrupulous persons started taking things and—get this—not paying for them honestly. One day, it was all working fine, thank you very much, and the next, Eaton's (a department store) was out of business, and it cost more to buy a cup of coffee than a litre of gasoline—although I think the last one is just at Starbucks. Anyway, the whole thing ended in a right old mess that really threw the country for a loop, which also ended up costing us because some computer nerd named Smiley Face :) had purchased the rights to public and country-wide loop throwing. A royal commission was called, which accomplished nothing except to force Canadians into following the rest of the world and using paper and coin forms of money. It was harder to get used to than the metric system, but I think it's finally caught on. Now we have corruption, money laundering and even counterfeiting on a scale that allows us to sit at the big boys' table. Many of us long for the good old days and worry that someday soon we may also be forced into using "restrooms," "flatware" or the phrase "uh-huh" in response to "thank-you."

But seriously…well, I hope you didn't think my little story above was true. It does, however, contain some near truths and semi-indirect lies. So, I can see where you might have been misled.

We have both paper money and coinage in Canada. The Royal Canadian Mint produces our coins. When I was in Ottawa visiting the mint as an adolescent, I saw one employee chasing another employee with a metal pipe in what can only be described as the unexpected and most memorable part of that tour. It has also been described as the beginning of a possibly violent fight. There's no official word from the mint on that though.

The Coins

All circulating Canadian coins have a portrait of Queen Elizabeth II on their obverse side.

The one-cent coin is the only circulating Canadian coin with a copper finish. It has two maple leaves on its reverse side and is commonly called a "penny."

The five-cent coin has a beaver on its reverse side. It has a silver finish and is slightly larger than the penny. It's most often called a "nickel."

The ten-cent coin has the smallest diameter of all circulating Canadian coins. It has a silver finish and bears a picture of the sailing schooner Bluenose on its reverse side. It's most often called a "dime."

The 25-cent coin is larger than the lower denomination coins. It's commonly called a "quarter" and has a picture of a caribou on its reverse side. Recently, Canadian quarters have been minted with various other scenes that replace the caribou, so don't panic if there isn't a caribou on yours. By the way, a caribou looks like a deer with really big antlers.

The 50-cent coin is a denomination that most Canadians don't see regularly. They are apparently minted and circulated, but I have never seen one. Most people would tell you that they haven't seen a Canadian 50-cent piece any time recently, so you're not likely to see one either. The 50-cent piece has the Canadian coat of arms on its reverse side, is finished in silver and is only smaller than the toonie in diameter.

The dollar coin is gold in colour and is commonly called a "loonie." It is larger than a quarter but smaller than a 50-cent piece or "toonie."

The two-dollar coin is bimetallic and is commonly called a toonie because that rhymes with loonie. It is the largest of Canada's circulating coins.

Bank Notes

Our bank notes, or bills as they are more commonly called, come in a variety of colours and denominations. All of our bills are printed by the Bank of Canada. The rainbow hues of our notes have, of course, led to many Americans suggesting that Canadian money and Monopoly money are one and the same. I am here to tell you that is not true. Monopoly money is valued much more highly than Canadian money. If you believe that, please go monopolize yourself. Actually, I should let you know that much of the world has paper money that comes in a rainbow of colours. America is one of the few countries in which paper money is a single colour—green. A fast fact, please use it as you wish.

Canadian paper money comes in denominations of $5, $10, $20, $50 and $100, but it is never distributed in denominations of Catholic, Protestant, Muslim or Jewish. Each denomination of Canadian paper money also has the portrait of a Canadian political figure on the front and some sort of Canadian scene or montage on the back.

The five-dollar bill is brilliant blue and is faced with a portrait of Sir Wilfred Laurier, our first French-Canadian prime minister, who served from 1896–1911. The back of the five, or fin as it is often called, has various scenes of children playing. Hockey, tobogganing and ice-skating are represented along with a quotation from "The Hockey Sweater," a famous short story by Québec writer Roch Carrier.

The 10-dollar bill is purple and is faced with a portrait of our first prime minister, Sir John A. Macdonald, who served from 1867–73 and 1878–91. The back of the "ten" contains a montage of peace and remembrance including a Canadian peacekeeper (which may have to be changed the way the Harper government is proceeding), people observing a Remembrance Day service, doves and a wreath of poppies. The first verse of "In Flanders Fields" is reproduced on the bill. Canadian doctor, poet and soldier John McRae wrote the poem in 1915 at the Battle of Ypres:

> *In Flanders fields the poppies blow*
> *Between the crosses, row on row,*
> *That mark our place; and in the sky*
> *The larks, still bravely singing, fly*
> *Scarce heard amid the guns below.*

The 20-dollar bill is green and has a portrait of Queen Elizabeth II on the face. On the back of the twenty is a montage of art and culture with pictures of sculptures by Bill Reid. He is a sculptor of Haida (a West Coast First Nation) and European parents age. There is also a quote from Canadian writer Gabriel Roy.

THE FAMOUS FIVE

The 50-dollar bill is officially red, but it looks a lot more pink than red. It is faced with a portrait of William Lyon Mackenzie King, Canada's longest serving prime minister (1921–26, 1926–30 and 1935–48). The montage on the back contains many things Canadians don't know that much about. The one that most people should know is the quotation taken from the first sentence of Article 1 of the United Nations' Universal Declaration of Human Rights: "All human beings are born free and equal in dignity and rights." The first draft of that document was written by New Brunswick native John Peters Humphrey. There is also a representation of a statue of the "Famous Five," which stands on Parliament Hill in Ottawa and in Olympic Plaza in Calgary. These five Canadian women petitioned the Supreme Court of Canada to declare that women were persons. The Supreme Court denied the request, but the Five went to the Privy Council of Britain on appeal where their request was eventually granted.

The 100-dollar bill is brown and has a portrait of Sir Robert Borden on its front. Borden was Canada's prime minister from 1911–20. The back of the hundred shows a satellite map of Canada, a satellite, a satellite dish and a birch bark canoe. Sounds a bit like a bit of a mishmash, but it apparently all falls under the theme of exploration and innovation. Hey money designers, whatever floats your canoe!

CHAPTER ELEVEN

SEX, CANADIAN STYLE

It always seems to come down to sex, doesn't it? So, just what do you need to know about Canadian-style sex that will help you as a Reasonable Facsimile of a Canadian? Well, we have two sexes…or is it three, four, perhaps even five? You're going to have to figure it out on your own. Perhaps there are six. Engaging a friend might make your inquiry more fun, though. Enjoy!

*A true Canadian is one who can make love
in a canoe without tipping.*
–Pierre Berton

CHAPTER TWELVE

HOW TO WEAR THE CANADIAN FLAG...
AND LIVE TO TELL ABOUT IT

So, just how, when and where does one wear the Canadian flag in proper fashion? Well, the short answer is this: don't. We really aren't a "wearing our flag on our sleeves" kind of nation. In fact, we have only had our official national flag with the big red maple leaf since 1965. There are, however, three occasions when wearing the Canadian flag is acceptable. They are Canada Day, when Canada beats the United States at some sporting event and when you're travelling abroad.

Canada Day

For obvious reasons, wearing or waving the Canadian flag on the annual celebration of Canada's birthday is appropriate, and you won't be looked down on for doing so. But be careful; too much flag-waving will get you funny looks. Subdued, sly and slight flutters are the best way to go. You should appear as though you are waving it but almost as if you don't notice or care. Think about how Queen Elizabeth II waves to passing crowds from her royal carriage. She barely seems to move her

hand. This is how the Canadian flag should be waved. By the way, for those of you who may have forgotten, Canada's birthday is July 1, and we have been a country (or pseudo-country) since 1867.

Canada Beats the United States at a Sporting Event

Whenever a Canadian athlete or Canadian team beats an American athlete or American team at a sporting event, it is always appropriate to wave and/or wear the flag. On these occasions, which may seem surprisingly frequent to you but not us, you may wave the flag with all the gusto, bravado and dislocating shoulder action you can muster. You know, like Americans do when they win something.

Travelling Abroad

As you travel, so does the Canadian flag. It's not a law, but it's definitely a general rule. Canadians learned long ago that when they travel abroad, they get much better treatment if they are not mistaken for Americans. This probably started in Europe, but it has certainly spread around the world. We're thought to be more polite, less pushy and generally nicer than Americans, so when we're in a foreign land we generally get treated pretty well—definitely better than American travellers. This may also have something to do with the fact that people in foreign lands aren't that concerned with Canadians scoping out their lands as part of a pre-invasion strategy. With Americans, of course, they aren't so sure.

I was in Barcelona one time and not wearing my Canadian flag either pinned to my collar or sewn to my knapsack. A waiter was surprised to discover that I was Canadian. It wasn't that I was showing some definitive American trait; it was because, as he said, "Canadians always wear a red maple leaf." The proof is in the proverbial pudding, eh?

The one issue that has arisen over wearing the Canadian flag abroad is people other than Canadians have figured out the trick. In fact, I have been told by some officials I know in Washington, D.C., that this ruse of appearing Canadian may even be a common way for Americans to conduct espionage while abroad. I have no proof of this, but rumours persist. It also would not be the only time something like this has occurred. Agents of Israel's intelligence service, the Mossad, have been known to use and have been caught using fake Canadian passports in their efforts at espionage and/or assassination. The Canadian government and Canadians in general have been particularly upset at these Israeli abuses, because one of the few perks we get as Canadians is being treated well when we're abroad. We don't want anyone screwing that up.

So, if you're going to fake being Canadian when you're abroad, the least you (Americans or Mossad agents) can do is act like Canadians—don't be nasty, pushy or assassinatory. It's un-Canadian.

CHAPTER THIRTEEN

CANADIAN WEATHER

If in Doubt...

There will be a time, whether in an elevator or at a fancy ball where you're dressed as "Lucinda the Could-be Gay Witch of the North," where an awkward silence will arise. You know the moment I'm talking about, my friends: the moment where you panic and are grasping for something to say—something Canadian. But instead of a snappy Canadian *bon mot*, you will panic and blurt something out about Iraq or the President's policy on Guam or Starbucks raising its prices, and all of a sudden you'll have given yourself away as less than Canadian. You may even be identified immediately as American. There will go all of my hard work, up in smoke! Now, you really don't want to do that to me, do you? Of course you don't.

So here is the secret to getting out of every awkwardly silent situation where you are absolutely desperate for something to say. Talk about the weather. That's right, the weather. We all do it. In fact, all Canadians do it ad nauseum. There is never a moment or occasion where it is out of place. It will never be misconstrued as a faux pas or rude. Let's face it, most of the time the only exciting things that happen in Canada are weather related. The American TV sitcom *Murphy Brown* once encapsulated a Canadian news program thusly: "Moose loose. Moose caught. More snow. Goodnight."

Even Hollywood has sort of figured out the secret to being Canadian. It's all about the weather.

In what other country would you find a climatologist travelling the land as a latter-day weather guru? That's right, David Phillips is a senior climatologist with the Meteorological Service of Canada (MSC) who has become a genuine Canadian celebrity by talking facts, figures and all things weather-related. He has become as ubiquitous as the weather trivia calendar that he promotes. He's likeable enough, but certainly not exciting in the vein of Indiana Jones. When he talks weather, though, Canadians listen. So follow his lead and talk weather. It'll save you in every situation.

One note of caution, though. You should probably know something about the weather in the Canadian locale you are in. So, here's the secret to that. Take a look out a window. I find it's the simple things that trip people up. I'm not being condescending, really. Just helpful!

CHAPTER FOURTEEN

CANADIAN FISSION... SORRY, THAT'S FASHION, EH!

Most of what Canada has produced in terms of fashion really falls into the category of warm and fuzzy. It's really not surprising considering that it's a cold place much of the time. That's not to say that there aren't some big-name, big-time designers in or originally from Canada. They, of course, do what most big-name designers do: charge exorbitant prices for what appear to be fur-lined napkins that barely cover the nipples of emaciated runway models. Though, in their defence, research and development of said nipple-covering, fur-lined napkins does not come cheap, nor do emaciated runway models. So one has to feel for the poor Canadian fashionistas. One, two, three. Ahhhhhhh! Okay that's enough feeling sorry for them.

What follows are a bunch of fashion-related words that will keep your Aspiring Reasonable Facsimile of a Canadian from showing. And no one likes to see a naked one of those dangling in the breeze. You might want to make a note of that!

Fashion Words, Eh!

Anorak

It's Not: the singular form of a group of Noraks

It Is: a hard to wear, or at least difficult to put on, waterproof and windproof pullover. It was originally an Inuit garment made of fashionable sealskin, but ever since Bridget Bardot made seals undesirable in terms of wearing them—mainly because they won't lie flat, and they wrinkle easily, and you know how the French hate wrinkles—anoraks have been made of some synthetic fibre combination like aluminum and polyester.

Bunny Hug

It's Not: something old-time cocktail waitresses do to pathetic older gentlemen who hang out in bars.

It Is: a warm and cozy-hooded sweatshirt; also called a hoodie or a kangaroo jacket

Gotch, Ginch and Gonch

It's Not: the words that were cartoonishly flashed across the screen during the fight sequences of the campy '60s TV show *Batman*.

It Is: men's underwear, usually associated more with briefs than boxers. They are also known as "gotchies."

Housecoat

It's Not: a colourful garment designed and worn by females, in the motif of the Duckworths' house from Coronation Street with its blue cladding and all. The front door would normally be at zipper height. To really understand this incorrect explanation you have to know that Coronation Street is a very long-running British soap opera that airs three to 12 times per week on our own CBC TV network. The Duckworths' house on said program was decorated in blue cladding. So, that previous incorrect explanation is really hilarious now that it's been explained, right?

It Is: a bathrobe that is normally feminine in gender—that is, worn by a female—as opposed to a regular bathrobe, which can be worn by men or women, sometimes at the same time, though that's risqué even for us!

Lumber Jacket

It's Not: a coat made of softwood lumber because we got hosed by the NAFTA treaty and one of our own sold us down the river to get a deal at all costs, even if it means Canadians get screwed. Hey, Stephen Harper, does this ring a bell?

It Is: a red and black or green and black plaid flannel jacket that is most often warn by blue-collar workers, hosers or heavy-metal fans. They are sometimes called "mack jackets" as well, which is short for mackinaw.

Runners

They Aren't: a short-form name for deadbeat fathers.

They Are Also Not: the long strings of goo that result from a mucousy winter cold

They Are: running shoes or sneakers

Tuque or Toque

It's Not: the way a marijuana cigarette is smoked

It Is: a knitted winter hat. Sometimes it has a pom-pom on the top. It is pronounced *toohk* or *tyewk*, no matter how you spell it.

CHAPTER FIFTEEN

SPORTS
THE FAKIN' EH! WAY

One of the biggest myths surrounding sports and Canada is that our national sport is hockey. It is not, nor has it ever been... well sort of. Lacrosse was traditionally Canada's national sport, but in 1994, laws were changed to accommodate the fact that politicians and dummies also known as "hockeyheads" no longer wanted to be told they were wrong when they said that hockey was Canada's national sport. Instead of finding out what the national sport was, the hockeyheads had the law changed to what they thought the national sport was, is and should be. However, the joke's still on them, because the politicians put qualifiers on the designation, so the hockeyheads are still wrong. What the law now says is that hockey—that is, ice hockey—is Canada's national winter sport and lacrosse is Canada's national summer sport.

Lacrosse, for those of you who do not know, is a sport played by two teams in which all players use netted sticks to carry, catch and throw a hard rubber ball to score goals by getting the ball past a goalie and into a net. First Nations people originally played the sport, and they called it *baggataway*. It was adopted by the French and given the name lacrosse.

For the record, I have played both lacrosse and hockey in organized leagues. Also for the record, I think hockey is the stupidest sport ever invented. It may have been invented by bored British soldiers stationed in Kingston, Ontario, with the intention of helping them pass the long, harsh and cold winters. Personally, I could care less who invented it or when and where it was invented, and I doubt very much whether it helped British soldiers forget the harshness of the long, cold winter. How do I know that? Well, here's my own little story about ice hockey.

Dan's Ice Hockey Memories…

One of the most common—and I do mean both déclassé and ordinary—happenstances of most Canadian children's lives is a strange obsession that parents have with organized team sports. My father was no less obsessed, though mercifully he focused his attentions more on my older brother. When I was six or seven years old, I was forced to join a hockey team and get up at 3:00 AM or some other ungodly hour. My brother and I laced up our skates and were forced to join a bunch of other kids on a team ingeniously named the Leafs. In dead of winter, at -80° or some horrid temperature, we headed to the outdoor rink behind Inch Park Arena on Hamilton's mountain. For six hours, or perhaps just one, we faced off against another team of shivering boys on a rink that was half of the official size. I guess they decided to give us a break and not make us skate on an official-size rink because we were so little. Perhaps they should have thought it through just a bit more so we could have skated on an indoor rink and not gotten frostbite on our toes, which for some reason snapped off inside our skates. Do you know what it feels like for your frostbitten toes to snap off? Well, I don't either, but it was really close.

Anyway, I couldn't tell you who won, though I do remember I was the goalie during the first game. I was the goalie because I couldn't skate, and in someone's inimitable wisdom (perhaps mine) being goalie seemed the position least likely to require skating skills.

Apparently, that wisdom does not hold true, because after that first game, I was no longer the goalie. I ended up being a defenceman, though I don't think I spent a lot of time defending anything. All I really remember is trying to figure out how I might get out of heading to that torturous rink every Saturday morning.

Mercifully, I only played ice hockey for one year. I played lacrosse for many years. Lacrosse was a better sport because it requires less skill, at least in terms of strong ankles for skating. However, the idiocy with lacrosse is that it's similar to hockey in terms of wearing all that equipment, but it takes place in the heat of summer. So basically, you sweat to death! Why not just shoot kids instead of torturing them like that? When I say kids, I mean me as a kid, not kids in general for those of you who have somehow misconstrued my thoughts and think that I think we should shoot kids. I was being sarcastic.

Anyway, I give you this, my dear Aspiring Reasonable Facsimile of a Canadian, as a sample of Canadiana that you may use at your will in terms of your fakery. By the way, I also have an

autographed picture of Paul Henderson—he's the guy who scored the winning goal in the Canada–Russia hockey series way back in 1972—for any of you hockey aficionados who may want to offer me something for it. I'd be more than willing to give it up if the price is right. Finally, I'd be finished with everything hockey!

Oh, and by the way, you should probably know the names Bobby Orr, Wayne Gretzky and Rocket Richard. They were all

WAYNE GRETZKY

great NHL hockey players at one time or another. You should also remember that the seminal event in Canadian hockey was the Canada–Russia hockey series in 1972, when Canadian NHL players defeated the Russians, but the Russians dispute that.

Then There's the Canadian Football League

I would be remiss if I didn't say something about the CFL. It's just like the NFL except that it has four downs instead of three, the playing field is larger (110 yards long by 65 yards wide) and it takes place in Canada. The team names are different— Montréal Alouettes, Toronto Argonauts, Hamilton Tiger Cats, Winnipeg Blue Bombers, Saskatchewan Rough Riders, Calgary Stampeders, Edmonton Eskimos and BC Lions—but the league is full of mostly American players.

I Guess I Have to Mention Curling

Curling is essentially shuffleboard on ice. I'm sure curlers would be offended by the over-simplification; however, calling it a sport seems to me an over-glamorization. Let's face it, any sport that can be played while someone is drinking beer does not inspire me to think of its participants as elite athletes. As proof, let us not forget that the oldest gold-medal–winning Olympian is a 49-year-old curler from Canada. Now, this category of sport should also include bowling and darts. I was going to go into an explanation of curling, however, shuffleboard on ice pretty much does it. You'll see curling all over CBC TV sports coverage. There are also a great number of Canadians who love the sport. The championship is held in a different place each year and is called the Brier.

Other Fakin' Eh! Sports

We play other sports in Canada, but for the most part they are just like the ones Americans play, so don't worry your pretty little head about it! Unless you're into the sport of "Pretty-Little-Head Worrying," which if you are, man you are twisted!

CHAPTER SIXTEEN

ARTSY FARTSY AND COLIN MOCHRIE

Let's start with Colin Mochrie. He is a very funny Canadian comedian who starred on the American improvisational comedy show *Whose Line Is It Anyway*. As a Reasonable Facsimile of a Canadian you should also know that Colin Mochrie starred in the British version of the same show, which preceded the American version by a number of years and did not star Drew Carey but also saw appearances by Ryan Stiles and Greg Proops.

The purpose of the above paragraph is to show that in terms of Canadian culture, you should probably look elsewhere. That is, somewhere other than in Canada. Well, it's not entirely true. You can look in Canada, and there are a lot of attempts made, but generally speaking, Canadians look elsewhere for their cultural entertainment. We do look at Canada for the types of cultural things that are good for us and paid for by us, but generally speaking are slow moving, earnest and really trying hard to be something or other.

Now you need to take this previous paragraph with a grain of salt, or perhaps Metamucil, depending on how everything is flowing, if you know what I'm saying. Generally speaking, the previous paragraph is how we Canadians look at our own culture. So for faking Canadian purposes, it's how you should look at it as well. This does, of course, make things excessively easy for you in that you are once again not going to have to do a whole lot of extra work in terms of looking at what makes up Canadian culture and the arts.

Broadcasting, Canadian Style

Can-con, meaning Canadian content, has been a cultural policy in Canada since the 1960s. The purpose of Canadian content regulations was to ensure that there would be a place on

Canada's airwaves for our own music, comedy, drama and news and that broadcasters wouldn't just air American programming. The concept has been highly successful in radio, and the Canadian music industry is truly thriving. In terms of news, Canada also has a thriving TV and radio news industry. In fact, the big stars of Canada tend to be TV news anchors. In terms of drama and comedy, there has been some success in radio, but in television, broadcasters have tended to spend most of their money on buying American shows. Canadian TV broadcasters are raking in buckets full of money thanks to their American produced shows, and they really only pay lip service to Canadian content with small budgets and most often bad timeslots.

Occasionally, there is a Canadian TV success story in terms of drama and more rarely in terms of comedy, but by and large, these are few and far between, although sketch and improvisational comedy have been rather larger hits on Canadian TV in the last 30 years or so. Specialty channels, which arose in the 1990s, air more Canadian content and have had some success, but again, this is mainly in the news, documentary or reality genres. One Canadian broadcaster summed up Can-con this way: "It's the cost of doing business." Not a pleasure, a money-maker or even something they care about…just simply a cost. Is Canadian TV full of evil? I think it speaks for itself.

…I Got the Music in Me…

What you really need to know is the number of famous recording artists who are Canadian. Here goes: The Guess Who, Paul Anka, Gordon Lightfoot, Leonard Cohen, Celine Dion, Diana Krall, Guy Lombardo,

SARAH MCLAUGHLAN

Anne Murray, Barenaked Ladies, k.d. lang, Shania Twain, Ian and Sylvia Tyson, Bryan Adams, Oscar Peterson, Sarah McLachlan, Joni Mitchell, Blue Rodeo, Rush, Hank Snow, Neil Young, Avril Lavigne, Paul Shaffer, Alannis Morrisette and Nelly Furtado. Just to name a few.

You should also remember the name Stompin' Tom Connors. Stompin' Tom is a Canadian institution. He got his nickname because he had the habit of stomping the heel of his boot to keep the rhythm. He was born in New Brunswick and had a rather tough upbringing but made it through nonetheless. Out of that came some of the most quintessentially Canadian compositions you'll ever hear. There was a time that Stompin' Tom was considered kitschy or a bit of a joke, but no more. Some of his songs include "Sudbury Saturday Night," "The Hockey Song" and "Big Joe Mufferaw."

BRYAN ADAMS

Pop Goes the TV

Well, I don't think there's a lot left to say about how I feel about Canadian TV. In terms of what you need to know as an Aspiring Reasonable Facsimile of a Canadian, here goes. You could safely say that you never watch Canadian TV programs. I grew up never watching Canadian TV, except for children's shows like *Mr. Dressup* and *The Friendly Giant*. CBC has traditionally been the place to watch *Hockey Night In Canada* (that's the NHL) and, more often than not, CFL and Olympic coverage.

THE KIDS IN THE HALL

The CTV and Global TV networks have always catered to buying American programs. That's where they focus their attention, and that's mainly what you'll see on their dials.

TV Shows to Remember

SCTV is thought of by many people as the seminal comedy show in Canadian TV. It aired in the 1980s and for a time was even seen on NBC in the United States. Some of the comedians who came out of that show were Martin Short, Andrea Martin, Catherine O'Hara, Dave Thomas, Joe Flaherty, Eugene Levy and the big man, John Candy.

The Kids in the Hall was also Canadian. If you don't know who the performers are, don't worry about it. *Saturday Night Live*, (SNL) though not a Canadian show, was created and produced by Canadian-born Lorne Michaels. Many of the stars of SNL were also born in Canada. They include Dan Aykroyd, Martin Short, Mark McKinney and Mike Myers.

CODCO, *This Hour Has 22 Minutes* and *Rick Mercer Report* are all programs with Newfoundland roots, and they're funnier than the proverbial place called Hell! They are also reason to believe that the CBC can get something right besides *Hockey Night In Canada*. Remember the names Rick Mercer and Mary Walsh. They are both hilarious and will continue to show up on Canadian TV screens.

Coronation Street is a long-running British soap opera that airs on the CBC. It runs in a half-hour serialized format during the week and as a block on Sunday mornings. Interrupt and/or move this program, and Canadians get their backs up, protest and inundate the CBC switchboard with complaints. It gets quite ugly if Olympic or curling coverage pre-empts the show.

Mr. Dressup was a kids' show that aired on CBC from 1967–96 and starred an American-born performer named Ernie Coombs as Mr. Dressup. All Canadian kids watched Mr. Dressup, and he often went to his "Tickle Trunk" and pulled out costumes to dress up in. There was nothing weird or untoward in the Tickle Trunk. Mr. Dressup was joined by a number of puppets over the years, the most famous of which were Casey and Finnegan. Finnegan, by the way, was a dog. You should know that and that Casey was a little girl puppet. Though as a child I thought Casey was a little boy.

The Friendly Giant was another television show that all Canadian children watched. It was 15 minutes of very gentle fun starring a giant of a man named Bob Homme. Friendly was joined by Rusty, a harp-playing chicken that lived in a sack and Jerome, a giraffe with blue spots. They often played music together—Friendly on the recorder, Rusty on the harp and Jerome dancing. You should remember this show and the opening line: "Look Up. Look waaaaaayyyy up!"

Canadian Films

There really aren't any strictly Canadian-made films that you have to remember. Generally speaking they are crap, and if you go with that attitude, you'll get by just fine as a Canadian.

Some Canadian filmmakers you may have heard of include Norman Jewison (sometimes referred to as St. Norman of Aurora) and David Cronenberg. Jewison has made many films, but they would mostly be considered American films—*In The Heat of the Night*; *The Russians Are Coming, The Russians Are Coming;* and *Moonstruck*, in which Cher made an amazing transformation from a woman with some grey hair to CHER! It was nothing short of miraculous. David Cronenberg started out making small, weird cult films like *Scanners* but has gone on to make larger, mainly American-backed weird films like *Naked Lunch* and *Dead Ringers*. For a quintessentially Canadian film-maker, you might want to check out films by Atom Egoyan. I wouldn't suggest it, but they do give a clear indication of Canadian films and their pacing—deviant and slow.

Canadian Art and the Stone that Is Soap

Canadian artists have, generally speaking, not reached the levels of fame of your Picassos or Dalis—or even Dollys. However, we do have our own homegrown artists. As a Canadian, you would be hard pressed to name…any. The Group of Seven and Tom Thompson painted post-impressionist scenes of Ontario's Algonquin Park in the early 20th century. There were actually 10 members of the Group of Seven, but most Canadians could not tell you the name of a single one of them. Tom Thompson was an affiliate of the group. He died under mysterious circum-stances (or in a bumbling Inspector Clouseau moment) in 1917.

The only other art that is well known in Canada is that made by Native Canadians. Totem poles are something most people know are made by West Coast Natives. The other type of art First Nations people are known for are soapstone carvings, which are mainly produced by Inuit artists. These you will find ubiquitously in every gift shop across this fair land of ours. It's also what prime ministers and their wives use to fend off intruders when the RCMP have fallen asleep at their posts. Heavy, shiny and easy to swing, soapstone carvings are a burglar's nightmare! This actually happened to Prime Minister Chrétien and his wife.

Now, if you want to be a show-off, and, of course, you really don't, you could also mention a late West Coast artist named Emily Carr. Although she was not a Native artist, her work was heavily influenced by the First Nations people of BC.

Architecture...We Knows How to Build...

Oh yeah, we know how to build things, although to be honest the only two names to remember are Arthur Erikson and Raymond Moriyama. Erikson may be Canada's most celebrated architect. He designed the Bank of Canada building in Ottawa, the BC Provincial Law Courts in Vancouver and Simon Fraser University. You've probably seen Simon Fraser University. It is often used as a location in sci-fi movies because it sits on top of a mountain and is rather stark and futuristic looking. Raymond Moriyama has done some big architectural projects as well, including the Ontario Science Centre, the Bata Show Museum (which looks like a shoebox and houses a collection of shoes) and the Canadian War Museum in Ottawa.

A controversial Canadian-born architect you as Americans may know is a certain Douglas Cardinal. He has designed a number of structures in Canada, including the Canadian Museum of Civilization in Gatineau, Québec. He is, however, probably best known for being removed as the primary design architect of the National Museum of the American Indian before it was completed on the National Mall in Washington, DC.

I also have it on good authority that an up and comer in the architectural field is a certain Paul de Figueiredo.

They Put the Lit in Can-Lit, Eh!

MARGARET ATWOOD

Canadian literature has traditionally been the domain of Canada's elite—the privileged few. It also originally existed, and perhaps still does, only because it was funded by the government. Can-Lit was good for you, bleak and hard to read, and every Canadian kid hated it (and perhaps still does). This, what you are reading right now, although written by a Canadian-born individual, could never be misconstrued as Can-Lit.

Can-Lit has traditionally been the domain of Margaret Atwood, Margaret Laurence and anyone else named Margaret. On occasion, names like Timothy Findley (*The Wars, Not Wanted on the Voyage*), Michael Ondaatje (*The English Patient*) and Douglas Coupland (*Generation X*) also managed to slip in there, but to be part of the literati in Canada, you really have to be named Margaret. I'd like to say there's another way to get in, but I don't know of any.

As for you, my dear and trusted Aspiring Reasonable Facsimile of a Canadian, you should know the above names, but don't bother reading anything by any of the above. It's really not necessary. Although if you're feeling ambitious, go for Timothy Findley's *Not Wanted on the Voyage*. It's a rather amusing (and amusement is rarely done in Can-Lit) account of Noah and his family during the Great Flood. You might also want to check out anything by the late Mordecai Richler. He was a curmudgeon of a man to say the least, but he had a way of dabbling with his pen to create stories of such quality that few in Canada have ever achieved. He also loved to stick it to the separatists in Québec, and that made him more Canadian than anything.

CHAPTER SEVENTEEN

HOLIDAYS AND OBSERVANCES

Canadian holidays and observances mirror many of those in the United States, though some have different names or dates when they are observed. Now, we don't do this just to be different, difficult or childish, but because we are a separate and unique country. So there! Official holidays are called statutory holidays or "stats" in Canada and are officially applicable to federal government employees. Generally speaking, everyone gets a free day off on a stat. The stat holidays include:

- New Year's Day (January 1)

- Good Friday (the Friday before Easter)

- Victoria Day (Monday on or before May 24) in celebration of Queen Victoria's birthday, and as an extension, a celebration of our current monarch

- Canada Day (July 1) Canada's birthday

- Labour Day (first Monday in September)

- Thanksgiving (second Monday in October, not a November holiday), which is our celebration of the fall harvest, not of the pilgrims

- Remembrance Day (November 11) in remembrance of Canada's war dead. Remembrance Day is a holiday across the country, except in Ontario and Quebec, where it is observed, but we don't get the day off. And we're angry about it, although not angry enough to start a police action.

- Christmas Day (December 25)

- Boxing Day (December 26) is the day when shops sell off their excess Christmas stock. Boxing Day is not a stat holiday in BC, Manitoba, New Brunswick, Nova Scotia, PEI, Nunavut or Yukon, although it is mainly just retail employees who work that day. And they're pretty pissed about it, but not pissed enough to start a Box Rebellion.

- The first Monday in August is a provincial or civic holiday that goes by various names across most of Canada.

- Alberta observes Family Day on the third Monday in February

- The Northwest Territories observes National Aboriginal Day on June 2

- Québec celebrates St. Jean Baptiste Day on June 24

Part 3

Putting it All Together, or How to Get Down With Your Fakin' Eh! Self!

CHAPTER EIGHTEEN

BUILDING YOUR CANADIAN IDENTITY

Well, believe it or not, we're nearing the end of our journey together. You've already got all the information on what it is to be Canadian—from hat size to shoe size and everything in between. What's that? You don't remember the section on hat sizes or shoe sizes. Well, there wasn't a specific section on either, but all the information you need to know on Canadian hat sizes and shoe sizes is there. The smartest among you know exactly what I mean. It is those smartest among you that we will welcome with open arms into this humble homeland of ours. Heck, we'll even let in some of you who are less clever if we're in a good mood that day. Don't worry. We will be in a good mood that day, even if it is not readily apparent.

The key now is to take all the information you've been awarded and meld that with your own unique personality. More than anything, it comes down to believability. So, don't try to stretch yourself too much. You know what I mean. Stick to what you know, what you don't know and don't be too ambitious. That's right, I'm saying coast, and coast like you've never coasted before. Because the only way to be comfortable with being a fake Canadian is to believe that's what you are. Not just think it, but also believe it! You have to be almost fully psychopathic in your belief that you are a Canadian. That's how we do it. We don't just think it—we live as and are psychopathically Canadian.

If you're into sports, then know everything you already do about sports and supplement that with Canadian sports knowledge. Know who is important in Canadian sports, the movers, the shakers and how Canadian sports are different.

If you're into the arts, take what you already know and meld that with everything you can find out in terms of arts in Canada. My brief section on Canadian culture will give you a good start, but go to the Internet and you can find out everything you need there. If you're into literature but not much into film, well, go for Can-Lit and forget the film. It's probably a good guideline to follow anyway. Just learn the basics as I've already given them to you. You don't have to know why Canadian film is crap, just know you don't go see Canadian films because they are crap. That's what you'll tell people. Enough said!

You will have to know the basics of our history and be able to place where the provinces, territories and major cities are located—that would be the geography. You should know what the flag looks like, how the federal government is made up and the names of the major political parties. But if you don't know details about these things in your own country (I am not necessarily singling you out, Mr. Bush), then don't sweat it too much about Canada.

If you're not a nice person, you can make that work for you. Remember, Canadians are really only nice on the surface. Just learn to hold your wicked tongue until people walk away and can't hear you. You should try to remember various Canadian words, both pronunciation and spelling, but try to avoid "out" and "about" until you've been here for a time and studied how we really say those two. Study all the Canadian food-related words and emphasize, if not go and try everything Tim Hortons. Various drinking-related sizes and measurements should also not confuse you, though if some or most things metric give you pause, that is perfectly acceptable. Heck, it's probably even better that way. The faces on the money are important, but not crucial, though the nicknames of coins you should know like the back of your hand. Get to know the holidays in each month—for the months that have them—and join your newfound countrymen in counting down to them in an almost religious way…even though they are generally not religiously based. With sex you're on your own, but I'd suggest not staying that way. It's always more fun with a friend or two, but not necessarily together, or separately for that matter. Remember, whether you know it or not, weather is a lifesaver.

As I said in an earlier chapter, your best bet in terms of successfully Fakin' Eh! is to head to Ontario, and Toronto in particular. It's a big multiethnic place that's easy to disappear into. Just ask any number of criminals…if you can find them. Just kidding. You'll never find them. Why? Because the city where I live has often been called Toronto the Good. Ya think that's ironic?

If you do follow my "slipping into Toronto" model for Fakin' Eh! all you really have to do is take some of the things from my life experiences and use them as your own. You can say you're from Hamilton, you've lived in the States, and pick or choose any other bits you may want to use. I'm fine with that. Hey, I'm done with it. It worked for me. You could choose to live outside of Toronto and use my information in reverse. If you get your Ontario sitcom accent down pat, you can live anywhere from Ontario to the West Coast and just say you're originally from Ontario. Half the people out West are actually from Ontario, so you'll fit right in. I would suggest you avoid trying to fit into Québec or any of the Atlantic Provinces. If you insist on trying, you could attempt to say you're originally from Ontario, but that will get you strange looks, and you'll never be one of them. So what's the point?

How to Fake Your Way Across the Border

There is actually no faking necessary in getting across the border, the U.S.–Canada border, that is. If you want to live in Canada, just come across as if you're on vacation. No one will stop you. They probably won't even give you a second look. Some people may think that acquiring a fake Canadian passport or birth certificate is the way to go. I do not advise, nor will I condone, any such illegal activity—especially by Mossad or

CIA agents. If you have acquired a fake Canadian passport or birth certificate or are pretending to come across for a visit, the border crossing will be a breeze. I've crossed the border from Canada to the United States by car, train and plane and only had detailed questions asked twice. The key to crossing the border successfully and with the minimum of fuss is to be calm, quiet and act like an idiot. That's right, act like it's the first time you've ever done crossed a border. The border guards love it when people give them fake respect…as long as they don't know it's fake. Never get jumpy, never act surprised and always say "yes sir, no sir" or "yes ma'am, no ma'am" (or "yes, no" if you're unsure of the border guard's gender). Border guard gender is sometimes an issue, as is determining whether they are animate or inanimate beings. You'll understand when you get there. Play it cool and coast away!

Job Interviews

If you are forced into such a common pursuit as having to work and go through a job interview to allow you to work, just play it cool. Don't ever over-hype yourself by saying you're the best, the brightest or the only. Be kind and standoffish, show your work, never apologize and above all else be polite. Isn't that how it's done in the United States? No matter. That's the way it should be done here.

Social Situations

Either avoid them or make small talk about the weather.

Dealing with Intrusive Media Types

Don't get famous, cocky or showoffy, and the media won't be a problem.

The Second to Last Piece, the Penultimate Point, a Conclusion Before an End

As I wrote in the beginning of this book, my intention is to help those poor unfortunate American souls who have become disillusioned with their current government and countrymen. It is and has always been my sincerest desire to find a way to help those unfortunate souls. With that in mind, I leave you with this thought: if my American-born dog can pass as a Canadian, why can't you? Why can't you, indeed?

CHAPTER NINETEEN

THE FAKIN' EH!
FINAL EXAM

What, you didn't think there'd be a test? Well, it is multiple guess, so you should be fine. Remember to coast away and think like a dog! Answers on page 223.

1) *Which province is the birthplace of universal healthcare in Canada?*

   a) Alberta

   b) Ontario

   c) Saskatchewan

2) *Which of the following sports is sometimes described as shuffleboard on ice?*

   a) figure skating

   b) curling

   c) midget wrestling

3) *Which province is often referred to as Lotusland?*

   a) Prince Edward Island

   b) Saskatchewan

   c) British Columbia

4) *What Canadian holiday falls on or around May 24?*

   a) Memorial Day

   b) Remembrance Day

   c) Victoria Day

5) *What's the easternmost province in Canada?*

    a) Alberta

    b) Nova Scotia

    c) Newfoundland and Labrador

6) *Who scored the winning goal in the Canada–Russia hockey series in 1972?*

    a) Bobby Orr

    b) Paul Henderson

    c) Bobby Hull

7) *What is the largest city in Nova Scotia?*

    a) Peggy's Cove

    b) Halifax

    c) St. John

8) *What metric measurement is close to a yard?*

    a) kilogram

    b) metre

    c) centimetre

9) *What female name is a necessity if you want to be part of Canada's Can-Lit Literati?*

    a) Jezebel

    b) Delilah

    c) Margaret

10) *Which province contains an area called the Badlands where you'll find a lot of old bones?*

    a) Ontario

    b) Québec

    c) Alberta

11) *What is a two-four?*

    a) a case of beer

    b) Timbits

    c) a Canadian two-dollar coin

12) *What's the easternmost territory in Canada?*

    a) Nunavut

    b) Northwest Territories

    c) Yukon

13) *How many provinces are there in Canada?*

    a) 50

    b) 10

    c) 13

14) *What product name do Canadians use instead of facial tissue?*

    a) Kraft Dinner

    b) Chesterfield

    c) Kleenex

15) *Which province probably produces Canada's funniestpeople— intentionally funny people, that is?*

a) Alberta

b) Québec

c) Newfoundland

16) *If you encounter an awkward situation, what should you talk about in Canada?*

a) French–English relations

b) how stupid Stephen Harper is

c) the weather

17) *Which Canadian prime minister once said "The state has no business in the bedrooms of the nation"?*

a) Stephen Harper

b) Pierre Trudeau

c) Brian Mulroney

18) *What term is given to the leader of the government inprovinces and territories?*

a) Joe, eh

b) premier

c) CEO

19) *Which is the most westerly Canadian territory?*

a) Yukon

b) Northwest Territories

c) Nunavut

20) *The occasional pre-emption of what TV show causes havoc at the CBC?*

   a) *Coronation Street*

   b) *Mr. Dressup*

   c) *The Friendly Giant*

21) *Who was Canada's longest serving prime minister?*

   a) Robert Borden

   b) Joe Clark

   c) William Lyon Mackenzie King

22) *Which is Canada's only officially bilingual province?*

   a) New Brunswick

   b) Ontario

   c) Québec

23) *What colour is the Canadian five-dollar bill?*

   a) green

   b) purple

   c) blue

24) *What is the capital city of Alberta?*

   a) Edmonton

   b) Calgary

   c) Medicine Hat

25) *When did Canada sort of become a nation?*

   a) 1867

   b) after the Canada–Russia hockey series

   c) 1982

26) *What are the two main products sold by Tim Hortons?*

   a) tires and tow chains

   b) birthday cards and coffins

   c) coffee and doughnuts

27) *Which of the following terms do Canadians use to mean electricity?*

   a) watery stuff

   b) gasoline

   c) hydro

28) *Which Canadian political party is nicknamed the Tories?*

   a) the Liberal Party

   b) the Parti Québecois

   c) the Conservative Party

29) *Which province mainly got hosed by the Alaska Boundary Dispute resolution?*

   a) Prince Edward Island

   b) Manitoba

   c) British Columbia

30) *Which Canadian comedian starred on the show* Whose Line Is It Anyway?

   a) Martin Short

   b) Dave Thomas

   c) Colin Mochrie

31) *Which province has the common loon as its official bird symbol?*

   a) Ontario

   b) Québec

   c) Manitoba

32) *Who were the first Europeans to arrive in Canada?*

   a) French

   b) Vikings

   c) Portuguese

33) *What's a chinook?*

   a) a big blow-hard

   b) a type of fish

   c) all of the above

34) *During which of the following conflicts did Canada first declare war for itself?*

   a) Boer War

   b) World War I

   c) World War II

35) *In which province would you find the city Portage La Prairie?*
   a) Manitoba
   b) Saskatchewan
   c) British Columbia

36) *The model for the Fakin' Eh! system was:*
   a) a tree
   b) a dog
   c) an American person

37) *Which of the following is not one of the Maritime Provinces?*
   a) New Brunswick
   b) Newfoundland & Labrador
   c) Nova Scotia

38) *The CFL playing field is:*
   a) longer than the NFL playing field
   b) wider than the NFL playing field
   c) both of the above

39) *Who was Canada's first prime minister?*
   a) Pierre Trudeau
   b) Alexander Mackenzie
   c) Sir John A Macdonald

40) *What is Stompin' Tom Connors' claim to fame?*
   a) Olympic athlete
   b) politician
   c) musician

41) *What do you need to know about the ethnic makeup of Canada?*

   a) everyone is Caucasian

   b) the southern part of the country is mainly populated by African-Canadians

   c) a multicultural makeup of cities (especially Toronto and Vancouver) means there are lots of different ethnic restaurants, and I just love ethnic food!

42) *Which Great Lake is not in Canada?*

   a) Lake Erie

   b) Great Slave Lake

   c) Lake Michigan

43) *Which Canadian Prime Minister once sang a duet with Ronald Reagan?*

   a) Stephen Harper

   b) Jean Chretien

   c) Brian Mulroney

44) *Which of the following was not one of the original four Canadian provinces?*

   a) Prince Edward Island

   b) Ontario

   c) New Brunswick

45) *What type of artwork is often chosen by prime ministers to fend off intruders?*

   a) totem poles

   b) soapstone carvings

   c) Raymond Moriyama buildings

46) *Which Governor General was forced to watch the Queen powder her nose during a formal dinner?*

   a) Ed Schreier

   b) Jeanne Sauve

   c) Adrienne Clarkson

Answers can be found below…

So there you have it my friend—my hopefully complete Reasonable Facsimile of a Canadian. You're done! You've read it, studied it, even tested yourself on it. Now it's time to take it to the streets. Whether you head across the border to test your skills in a trial run or head on over with the intention of staying, do it with gusto! Dive headlong into it, mean it and believe it.

And please don't let anyone tell you that this whole thing was a ruse by the Ministry of Tourism to get more Americans to visit Canada. Because if it's one thing Canadians are, it's honest. Really! No, I mean it, really. Really I do. How many times do I have to say really to get you to really believe me? Five? Okay? Done!

Quiz Answers

1c, 2b, 3c, 4c, 5c, 6b, 7b, 8b, 9c, 10c, 11a, 12a, 13b, 14c, 15c, 16c, 17b, 18b, 19a, 20a, 21c, 22a, 23c, 24a, 25a, 26c, 27c, 28c, 29c, 30c, 31a, 32b, 33c, 34c, 35a, 36b, 37b, 38c, 39c, 40c, 41c, 42c, 43c, 44a, 45b, 46c

ABOUT THE AUTHOR

Dan de Figueiredo

Dan de Figueiredo has been a journalist, television writer, filmmaker and playwright. His love for words began when his aunt and uncle gave him a copy of Robinson Crusoe, and he never looked back. After earning his BA in Political Science at McMaster, followed by a BAA in Journalism from Ryerson, Dan worked on the Canadian edition of *Who Wants to Be a Millionaire*, *Reach for the Top*, numerous television and theatre productions and several independent films. He is currently a freelance television writer, producer and researcher, and he has written two other books for Blue Bike—*Weird Canadian Places* and *Weird Ontario Places*.

ABOUT THE ILLUSTRATOR

Roger Garcia

Roger Garcia immigrated to Canada from El Salvador at the age of seven. Because of the language barrier, he had to find a way to communicate with other kids. That's when he discovered the art of tracing. It wasn't long before he mastered this highly skilled technique, and by age 14, he was drawing weekly cartoons for the *Edmonton Examiner*. He taught himself to paint and sculpt; then in high school and college, Roger skipped class to hide in the art room all day in order to further explore his talent. Currently, Roger's work can be seen in a local weekly newspaper and in places around Edmonton.